TATES CREEK CHRISTIAN CHURCH
3150 TATES CREEK R?
LEXINGTON

SMALL
GROUP

H
E
L
P

GUIDES

Now th... good question!

by
Terry Powell

Standard®
PUBLISHING
Bringing The Word to Life

Cincinnati, Ohio

Now That's A Good Question!
Published by Standard Publishing,
Cincinnati, Ohio
www.standardpub.com

© 2007 by Terry Powell
All rights reserved. No part of this book may
be reproduced in any form, except for brief
quotations in reviews, without the written
permission of the publisher.

Printed in United States of America.

Design and production by Susan Lingo Books ™

All Scripture quotations, unless otherwise indi-
cated, are taken from the HOLY BIBLE, NEW
INTERNATIONAL VERSION®, NIV®. Copy-
right © 1973, 1978, 1984 by International Bible
Society. Used by permission of Zondervan
Publishing House. All rights reserved.

14 13 12 11 10 09 08 07   9 8 7 6 5 4 3 2 1
978-0-7847-2074-5

DEDICATIONS

*To the Family and Church
Education students at Columbia
International University, past
and present. You are my most
significant teachers who make
classroom discussion a learning
experience for me.*

*A hearty thanks to my editor,
Michael Mack, and to my agent,
Mary Sue Seymour. I appreciate
your encouragement!*

Personal Note

*Terry Powell is available for
training teachers or small group
leaders (803-754-4100 x3453 or
tpowell@ciu.edu)*

Contents

Introduction

PREVIEW OF COMING ATTRACTIONS

Can you identify with the following prayer?

> Dear God, so far today I've done all right. I haven't gossiped or lost my temper. I haven't cheated anyone out of money or stared at a beautiful woman with lust. I haven't been grumpy or selfish, and I'm really glad of that. But in a few minutes, Lord, I'm going to get out of bed, and from then on, I'm going to need all the help I can get. Amen.

Who doesn't need lots of help to make it through the day! "Help" is often the cry of small group leaders too. I've had my share of times when I needed counsel or a fresh idea. That's the purpose of this book: to help you in your significant role as a group leader.

The help you'll receive here relates to the "Bible discussion" aspect of your role. Together we'll explore the factors that affect group members' motivation and find ways to foster a hospitable group climate in which discussion thrives. You'll learn how to delve into God's Word for yourself to prepare for discussion. You'll discover how to ask questions so participants can observe, interpret, and apply the Bible. We'll illustrate the guidelines for questions that are educationally and biblically sound and then show you how to put your questions and study notes into a logical sequence on paper. Next we'll examine leader behaviors that improve the quality of group interaction and increase the number of people who participate in the discussion.

Perhaps this book will be the way God answers your cry for help. Before we go any further, let me explain what I mean by "Bible discussion."

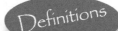

Definitions

Bible Discussion: Take the following definition to heart. By the time you finish this book, you'll know why it is crafted in this precise manner.

Effective Bible discussion, generated by a hospitable learning environment, is a guided conversation that involves people in observing, interpreting, and applying God's Word.

Of course, all Bible discussion should be done in prayerful reliance on the Holy Spirit to illuminate God's Word and guide the interaction. Beyond this, successful Bible discussions have at least six components:

➤ *A leader who originates and directs the conversation*

➤ *One or more questions to provoke thought*

➤ *A meaningful, specific goal for group interaction*

➤ *Two or more interested participants*

➤ *An authoritative source of truth (God's Word)*

➤ *A supportive learning environment*

In chapter 1 you'll learn how to accomplish the "hospitable learning environment" part of the definition.

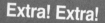

Extra! Extra!

If one of your roles is the point person for small groups in your church, be sure to read the Small Group HELP! Guide, Let's Get Started! How to Begin Your Small Groups Ministry, by Dan Lentz (Standard Publishing). If you're not the point person for groups in your church, this book makes a great gift for the person who is!

Creating a Climate for Discussion

A local advertising periodical offered the following disclaimer: *Just in case you find mistakes in this paper, please remember they were put there for a purpose. Some folks are always looking for mistakes, and we try to please everyone!*

In This Chapter...

- Caring atmosphere
- Value of humor
- Group intercession
- Variety in methods
- Assimilating guests
- Trait of transparency
- Physical environment

Now that's an original way to cover your tracks! Just make light of any failures somebody might spot. Then no one thinks twice about them. When it comes to making mistakes, we're all pros. But there's one mistake discussion leaders make to their own peril: taking the group's "learning atmosphere" or "feeling tone" for granted. We flirt with failure when we're insensitive to the factors that either stimulate or stifle folks' participation.

This chapter advances the principle that effective Bible discussion depends on a warm, hospitable climate. If the environment is cool, impersonal, or unsafe, discussion fizzles, no matter how sound the questions are that we ask. What follows are seven strategies for creating a climate that fosters sizzling interaction.

CARING

My wife and I were in our mid-20s when we joined our first small group Bible study. We became fast friends with others in the group. When one of us had a problem or faced a challenge, we knew we could count on the others. When we moved out of state a year later, I wept because of the bond that would be broken.

The first critical factor in establishing a motivational climate is caring. When leaders show genuine interest in people and when group members put a premium on relationships, Bible discussions receive a boost. Participants are more likely to interact when they know others in the room accept and care about them.

The interpersonal dimension of a Bible-teaching ministry was paramount to the apostle Paul. While reminiscing about his ministry among the Thessalonians, he wrote, "We loved you so much that we were delighted to share with you not only the gospel of God but our lives as well, because you had become so dear to us" (1 Thessalonians 2:8).

Here are ways to facilitate a caring environment:

For more on the interpersonal dimension of leading small groups, see the Small Group HELP! Guide, *Who, Me . . . a Leader? How to Guide an Effective Small Group*, by Michael Mack (Standard Publishing). This guide shows how to cultivate the internal qualities of a Christ-like leader, based on Jesus' leadership of his small group.

➤ *Pray for the Holy Spirit to create a strong bond among group members.* Cultivating close fellowship is a spiritual endeavor, not solely the result of human effort.

➤ *Ask the Lord to give you love for each person in the group, especially those whose temperaments or idiosyncrasies tend to get on your nerves.* Then ask him to show you concrete ways to express that love. One strategy is to pray regularly for them. God often changes our attitude toward people when we intercede for them. And let them know you're praying for them.

➤ *Be the first to arrive at the meeting site and greet people as they enter.* Ask them questions about their week or follow up on something they said in the previous session. I'm an introverted, task-oriented person, but I still shower people with attention when they enter the room. I force myself to do it, even when I don't feel like it, because it sets a positive tone for the session. I won't allow my fluctuating emotions to control me.

➤ *Be sure you or someone in the group calls anyone who misses a session.* Don't harass them for not attending; just let them know they were missed.

➤ *Send handwritten notes in the mail to encourage participants.* Salute someone who exhibits enthusiasm for learning or has a big appetite for

God's Word. Thank a group member whose transparency took a lot of courage. Express gratitude to someone who comforted a hurting group member.

➤ *Plan and implement a Bible study on authentic fellowship.* As a group, examine the Bible passages in the box and discuss these questions: *What expressions of fellowship can we glean from these verses? Who can share a time when you've been on the receiving end of one of these forms of fellowship? What are some hindrances to experiencing fellowship of this sort? How can we demonstrate these forms of fellowship within our group?*

➤ *When you form a new group, don't delve into Bible content right off the bat.* Employ get-acquainted or team-building activities to increase folks' comfort level with each other. See the Team-Building sidebars scattered throughout this book.

The Word on Leading Discussions

"Carry each other's burdens, and in this way you will fulfill the law of Christ" (Galatians 6:2).

"Therefore encourage one another and build each other up, just as in fact you are doing" (1 Thessalonians 5:11).

"Let the word of Christ dwell in you richly as you teach and admonish one another with all wisdom, and as you sing psalms, hymns and spiritual songs with gratitude in your hearts to God" (Colossians 3:16).

"Be completely humble and gentle; be patient, bearing with one another in love" (Ephesians 4:2).

"Be kind and compassionate to one another, forgiving each other, just as in Christ God forgave you" (Ephesians 4:32).

"Be alert and always keep on praying for all the saints" (Ephesians 6:18).

"Be devoted to one another in brotherly love. Honor one another above yourselves" (Romans 12:10).

"Rejoice with those who rejoice; mourn with those who mourn" (Romans 12:15).

"Accept one another, then, just as Christ accepted you, in order to bring praise to God" (Romans 15:7).

"Each one should use whatever gift he has received to serve others, faithfully administering God's grace in its various forms" (1 Peter 4:10).

LAUGHTER

Humor surfaces normally when folks enjoy being together. Don't feel constrained to collect an arsenal of jokes and fire a volley at the group each week. It is wise, however, to plant a humorous anecdote in a study when you can connect it to a concept or principle from a Bible passage.

TRY THIS!

Ask group members to select one item from their wallet or purse to use in introducing themselves or to disclose personal information, such as a photo, receipt, or business card. Give everyone time to display and explain the items. Encourage others to ask probing questions that elicit even more information.

I once led a sobering lesson on the evidence of moral erosion in King Solomon's life. The older he got, the more foolishly he acted. To introduce this high-profile exception to the "older is wiser" rule, I offered a few telltale signs of aging.

You know you're growing old when...

- *you sink your teeth into a steak...and they stay there*
- *your back goes out more than you do*
- *you lean over to pick up something off the floor, and you start wondering, now what else can I do while I'm down here?*
- *you sit in a rocking chair and can't make it go*
- *you turn the lights out for economic rather than romantic reasons*

Next, I made a clear transition into Solomon's later years. Laughter is a social lubricant for the learning environment. The absence of appropriate humor in small group interaction settings may be an indicator of poor bonding.

WiSe Words

"I have lost count of the times I have stood before an audience that was hostile to the message of Christ, only to see their hearts made soft and receptive by the appropriate use of humor. Whether the audience is six or sixty, humor can break down barriers that almost nothing else can."
—Ken Davis, *Secrets of Dynamic Communication*

Humor also aids retention of content you're covering. Researchers tested two different college classes six weeks after they received the same lecture from the same professor. One class received several humorous anecdotes that related to the material while the other didn't. Students who had heard the humor-laced presentation remembered more (Debar Korobkin, "Humor in the Classroom," in College Teaching).

How does humor improve recall of information? Humor is graphic and causes a visual image to appear in the mind. Images are easier to remember than abstract ideas or mere words.

The Internet teems with clean humor. You can also peruse the shelves in the humor section of a bookstore. My favorites are Richard Lederer's Anguished English and More Anguished English and Jay Leno's series on true but ridiculous headlines. It's OK to share humorous stuff once in a while, even when it doesn't tie into your Bible study. There's truth to the old adage that humor breaks the ice and heats up the atmosphere.

Caution

Exercise sensitivity in your use of humor. What you say shouldn't make anyone look bad, whether or not the person is part of your group. Don't belittle any ethnic group or nationality. Any joke you tell should be acceptable to you if you heard it from your child or teenager. But it's usually OK to poke fun at yourself! The person who learns to laugh at himself will never cease to be entertained.

INTERCESSION

I once heard intercession defined as "rebellion against the status quo." To pray for your group members and to reserve meeting time for them to pray for one another acknowledges dependence on the Holy Spirit. It shuttles them from the "spiritual status quo" to greater Christlikeness. Folks who bear each other's burdens in this manner will feel free to ask or respond to questions during a Bible study.

Consider the following ways to enhance the ministry of intercession within your group.

➤ **Tag the following questions onto the end of your Bible studies:** *What personal needs has the Holy Spirit exposed during this study? How can we pray with you about those needs?*

➤ **Link times of intercession to lesson application.** In a study I led on "The Ministry of Encouragement," everyone shared with a partner the names of persons who were experiencing discouraging circumstances. After brainstorming for concrete, realistic ways to encourage those in need, everyone prayed for his partner to follow through on at least one idea. If you have a close-knit group, ask everyone to huddle with one or two others before dispersing. They can discuss application ideas and pray for each other's follow-through.

➤ **Lead a Bible study on the theme of intercessory prayer.** Examine the biblical basis for this expression of group life and discuss ways to exercise intercession in relation to one another. Scripture is chock-full of references to intercession. For instance, my title for Nehemiah 1 is "The Ministry of Intercession." The following questions directed learners into the passage and encouraged application:

1. *What need prompted Nehemiah's intercession?*

2. *What needs of people in our phase of life should prompt our prayers for one another?*

3. *Based on Chapter 1, what qualities did Nehemiah possess?*

4. *Why are those traits essential to intercession?*

5. *What can we learn about intercession from Nehemiah's prayer in verses 5-11?*

6. *What insights from Nehemiah 1 are most applicable to our relationships within this group?*

WiSe WorDs

"If we truly love people, we will desire for them far more than it is within our power to give them, and this will lead us to prayer. Intercession is a way of loving others."

—*Richard J. Foster, Prayer: Finding the Heart's True Home*

➤ **Model the level of personal disclosure you want group members to reach.** Share prayer requests of your own that are personal, reveal a struggle, and show your dependence on the body of Christ for support.

➤ **Distribute a list of all group members' e-mail addresses.** Encourage everyone to e-mail all the others the day they become aware of a group member's illness or special need. This way they can start interceding before the next gathering of the group.

METHODOLOGY

A mom asked her first-grader, "What did you learn in school today?" A frown creased his face as he replied, *"Nothing. The teacher teached and teached so much I didn't have time to learn anything!"* A variety of methods is important for all ages. Bible discussion flourishes in a small group or class where participatory methods are the norm, not the exception.

The more consistently we involve learners, the more successful any attempt at discussion will be. If we pop a question out of the blue to a group accustomed to straight lecture, we'll likely receive limited responses. Yet in a group where a mix of methods is routine, what happens when we pose the same question? The room buzzes with dialogue! Involve your group members with a variety of approaches, and watch the learning atmosphere heat up.

What prompts me to strive for variety in my discussions is the *predictability principle.* Howard Hendricks suggests that the more predictable one's teaching methodology, the lower the impact on learners. The less predictable one's choice of learning activities, the greater the impact (Color Outside the Lines).

You also need guidelines for determining which method to employ for a particular lesson or group. Here are a few questions I ask myself when I'm trying to decide which learning activity to employ or how to adapt published lesson plans:

- *How should the nature of this Bible passage affect my choice of methods?* Is some of the material so complex or controversial that I need to set the stage for discussion with a brief lecture?

- *How does the location where my group meets affect the choice of learning activities?* Is there enough space to sit in a circle or divide into smaller buzz groups? Will a particular approach disturb a group that's meeting nearby? How do I adapt a lesson I've taught in Sunday school to the more informal setting of the den in my home?

- *How does my time limit affect the approach I take for this study?* Should I substitute one discussion strategy for another that will take less time?

- *Which approach is most likely to facilitate a hospitable climate and get members interacting with each other, not just with me as the leader?*

- *Will my methods and questions enable group members to experience all three phases of Bible study: observation, interpretation, and application?* (Chapters 2–4 equip you to ask questions corresponding to all three phases of study.)

- *What activities are most appropriate for my particular group?* How does group size, age, level of spiritual maturity, educational background, or amount of small group experience affect their degree of receptivity to particular strategies or questions?

- *Am I comfortable implementing a method I've never tried before?* Am I confident it will succeed, or do I fear that it will flop? (I want to expand my horizons and try new things, yet I need to believe in a learning activity for it to succeed.)

ASSIMILATION

How well does your group assimilate new people? Find out by answering these questions:

✔ **What percentage of guests attending my group return?**

✔ **How frequently do newcomers drop out after a few weeks or months?**

✔ **What words describe the behavior of "regulars" toward visitors?**

✔ **What strategies do I employ to cultivate a sense of belonging and improve assimilation?**

✔ **How do we follow up and make contact with a person after he or she visits the first time?**

Definition: Assimilate

To absorb into a system or into the cultural tradition of a particular group of people. Assimilation occurs in a small group or class when a visitor feels welcome and quickly shifts from marginal commitment to consistent participation.

Right after a new person or couple joins your group is a good time to implement another team-building activity. Select one that expedites the learning of everyone's name.

SUPER-SIZE IT!

Recruit an outgoing "class host or hostess" for the Sunday school class you teach. This person's ministry is vital to establishing a warm, hospitable environment in a large class. The role alleviates the pressure on you as a Bible-discussion leader and allows you to concentrate on the day's study. Here are several things this person can do:

Arrive early and greet any visitors to the class, then introduce them before the Bible lesson starts

Circulate a sign-up sheet so different class members can bring refreshments from week to week

Update the class about members who are sick

Elicit "news and prayer requests" from members, which lead to a short period of intercession

Ask everyone to think of three -ing words that disclose personal information. (A chef might think of "cooking." An insurance agent might opt for "selling." A new member of Weight Watchers might choose "dieting.") Have every member of your small group share these words with the others. If you teach a large Sunday school class, turn it into a mixer. Tell everyone to meet three folks they don't know well, and then use the -ing words as a means of introduction.

TRANSPARENCY

Sometimes the pivot on which a good Bible discussion turns is the leader's transparency. Transparency takes the form of sharing a personal illustration or asking participants to intercede on your behalf. What happens when you add a personal dimension to your leadership? You send positive messages to group members.

> ➤ *"What we're studying has encouraged or convicted me."*

> ➤ *"This has been prepared in my heart, not just my head."*

> ➤ *"I'm not self-sufficient. I need to lean on Christ daily, and I need others in the body of Christ."*

Genuinely identify with learners or come across as real, and you've found the key to their hearts.

Thirty interviews with Bible college students unveiled to me the power of revealing personal experiences. In my doctoral dissertation research, I asked students to describe behaviors of faculty members that improve student-faculty relationships. What they shared also applies to Bible-study settings. Twenty-six out of thirty mentioned transparency as a positive teaching trait leading to nonclass-room student-teacher interaction! I heard these kinds of phrases often:

The Word on Leading Discussions

The apostle Paul modeled transparency before the people he led: "We do not want you to be uninformed, brothers, about the hardships we suffered in the province of Asia. We were under great pressure, far beyond our ability to endure, so that we despaired even of life. Indeed, in our hearts we felt the sentence of death. But this happened that we might not rely on ourselves but on God, who raises the dead.... On him we have set our hope that he will continue to deliver us, as you help us by your prayers" (2 Cor. 1:8-11).

> ➤ *"When a teacher shows the down side of himself"*

> ➤ *"When they share personal experiences"*

> ➤ *"When an instructor talks about his own problems in daily living for God"*

One student echoed the sentiment of others when he said, "It shows that a teacher understands what I'm going through." Another respondent remembered his youth ministry professor's testimony about a time she was "disappointed with God" and didn't feel connected to him. "I was having trouble with the same thing," he reported, "and I could relate to her and we talked about it."

Should a leader publicize every secret she's ever shared with God? No. Divulge every private sin that's ever plagued him? Of course not! Be discreet about what you say. Don't feel you have to show all your failings to others in the group. Before choosing what personal things to share, think about these six guidelines:

6 GUIDELINES FOR PERSONAL SHARING

Will my personal anecdote accelerate Bible application by clarifying a truth we're covering?	Will self-disclosure meet a genuine need in my life for emotional support and prayer?
Will my personal illustration show either the benefits of obeying a particular truth, or the painful consequences of neglecting it?	Will my illustration portray family members or friends in a negative manner?
Will my self-revelation encourage others to share needs and prayer requests?	Have I received permission to tell the story from people who could be embarrassed by it?

"Our earthiness must be as apparent to others as the power is, so they may see that the secret is not us, but God. That is why we must be transparent people, not hiding our weaknesses and failures, but honestly admitting them when they occur."
—*Ray Stedman, Authentic Christianity*

Although you should be selective in your sharing, transparency is an in-your-face slam dunk against hypocrisy and superficiality in a group.

Also strive to promote transparency among your group members. Perhaps the wisest approach is to ask for personal reactions to the Bible lesson you're covering. In any given session, I may employ just one or two questions. I reserve questions of this sort for the final minutes of a study. Here's a list of questions that have been successful for me:

- *What personal application or carry-over idea has the Lord given you from this study?*
- *What personal need or issue has the Holy Spirit exposed during this study? How can we pray with you about it?*
- *Who can illustrate one of our lesson truths from your personal experience?*
- *What fresh, I-never-thought-of-that-before insight did you glean from today's Scripture?*

- *As we identified timeless truths in today's lesson, perhaps a positive role model came to mind. If so, tell us about this person. How did he or she apply or demonstrate some point we covered?*
- *What unresolved questions on this subject matter still goad you?*

ENVIRONMENT

The nature of your surroundings—your physical environment—affects the learning climate. Years ago I read a study showing the correlation between the quality of relationships among members of deacon boards and their meeting location. Those who met in homes, with softer seating and more informal surroundings, reported deeper-level friendships and more meaningful intercession among members than the boards who met at church (Church Administration). What can you do to make your meeting place more hospitable?

If you want to "think outside the box" and be really creative, try the "rotation principle." Periodically change the meeting location so it fits the theme of your Bible study. Let these examples serve as catalysts for your thinking.

- ✳ **Launch a series on Philippians from an empty jail cell. Paul wrote from prison and demonstrated joy despite confinement.**
- ✳ **Discuss God's creativity from Genesis 1 or Psalm 8 during an outdoor picnic.**
- ✳ **To explore the role of discipline in spiritual growth, meet in a gym or exercise room. Cite parallels between discipline in the physical and spiritual realms.**

* Go to a cemetery to examine texts on the brevity or uncertainty of life (Ps. 39:4-6; 49:5-12; 90:10-12, or James 4:13-15). **Or use the same site to study 2 Timothy 4, where Paul gave his "last will and testament" before his impending death.**

* **Meet in the conference room of a bank for a Bible study on money.**

* **Start a series on parenting by sitting on the carpet in your church's nursery.**

What message does your meeting location convey?

Do the cleanliness, décor, and seating arrangement provide a welcome mat?

Are refreshments provided to help achieve an informal atmosphere?

Is the room temperature too stuffy or uncomfortably cool?

Is interaction enhanced by a seating arrangement where everyone can see other's faces?

SUPER-SIZE IT!

If space permits, try a U-shaped layout in your youth or adult class-room. This allows all participants to see each other and promotes an interchange of ideas. You can still sit in front, with a marker board behind you for use. Your spot still connotes a measure of authority and control if you consider that important. You can switch between standing and sitting during the lesson, as needed. There's an added advantage if everyone sits around tables. Tables provide learners a natural protec-tion against the discomfort some may feel about sharing. They feel less exposed, less vulnerable to peers' analysis of their ideas. This is especially true for teens.

BRINGING IT HOME

Seven words provide an organizational framework for this chapter, representing strategies for creating a group climate that stimulates discussion.

CARING: Show concern for group members and work to enhance their relationships with each other.

LAUGHTER: Weave discreet humor into your meetings.

INTERCESSION: Make prayers for one another a priority.

METHODOLOGY: Vary your approach to discussions.

ASSIMILATION: Make visitors feel welcome and accepted.

TRANSPARENCY: Model the kind of openness you want to see in the group.

ENVIRONMENT: Prepare your meeting place so it's warm and hospitable.

The first letter of each word forms an easy-to-remember acronym: C-L-I-M-A-T-E. You don't have to be a meteorologist to keep tabs on the climate in your group.

Getting Into God's Word

Here's one of my favorite stories:

A small bottle containing urine sat upon the desk of Sir William Osler, the eminent professor of medicine at Oxford University. Sitting before him was a class full of young, wide-eyed medical students, listening to his lecture on the importance of observing details. To emphasize his point, he announced: "This bottle contains a sample for analysis. It's often possible by tasting it to determine the disease from which the patient suffers."

He then dipped a finger into the fluid and brought a finger into his mouth. He continued speaking: "Now I am going to pass the bottle around. Each of you please do exactly as I did. Perhaps we can learn the importance of this technique and diagnose the case."

The bottle made its way from row to row, each student gingerly poking his finger in and bravely sampling the content with a frown. Dr. Osler then retrieved the bottle and startled his students by saying, "Students, now you will understand what I mean when I speak about details. Had you been observant, you would have seen that I put my index finger in the bottle and my middle finger into my mouth."

—from Wayne Rice, Hot Illustrations for Youth Talks

Just as close observation of a patient is integral to diagnosis, observing details is also crucial to Bible study. In fact, it's the first of three phases of Bible study: observation, interpretation, and application.

In this chapter I'll define each phase and suggest a method for implementing each in your preparation for Bible discussions. I know you're busy. You won't have time to implement all these steps before every Bible study you lead. But when you do, your enthusiasm will skyrocket because you'll be sharing original insight rather than somebody else's research. These strategies will enhance your devotional study of Scripture too. If God has given you an appetite for his Word, this chapter will show you how to feed yourself. It will also prepare you to ask the kinds of Bible study questions recommended in chapters 3 and 4.

TEAM BUILDING

Each week your group meets, reserve five minutes for an interview with one of the participants. If your group size is typical, you should cover everyone in two to three months. The questions you ask should vary somewhat from person to person, but here are a few to spur your thinking:

Where did you live between the ages of 5-10?

Tell us about your all-time favorite vacation.

What do you enjoy doing on your days off?

"If you had an email waiting for you, who would you want it to be from and what would you want it to say?"

Who was most responsible for you coming to Christ?
(Avoid if you're not sure of someone's salvation)

How can we pray for you right now?

FOCUSING ON FACTS

Observation is the important starting point in your Bible study. Timeless truths and their application are only as sturdy as their factual foundation. We're less likely to misinterpret Scripture when we base our conclusions on what the passage says.

When you lead your group, you'll want to give participants observation assignments or questions so they can see important facts. The more facts you discover in your preparation, the easier it will be to ask observation questions.

Definition: Observation

The close inspection of a Bible passage, usually resulting in a written record and classification of facts. It's more than just reading. It's close scrutiny demanding focused attention.

Here's a maxim that captures this phase of Bible study: If you're looking for something, you're more likely to find it. Pretty self-evident, huh? But it refers to the importance of intentionality in your examination of a passage. The key to observation is to know what to look for, to be aware of the kinds of factual information that most often crop up in God's Word. Then you go on an expedition and look for those passage elements.

WHAT TO LOOK FOR

What follows are *observation cues*. Each is a signal to look for a particular kind of factual information. I recommend that you put these observation categories on an 8 ½ x 11 sheet of paper, designed like the layout on page 24. Abbreviate what you write as much as possible. This chart works best if you use it with no more than one Bible chapter and no less than a single episode or long paragraph. Occasionally, you'll need more space for some columns than a one-page chart provides. When you use this approach, you'll see how the observation cues pull passage elements toward you like iron filings to a magnet. Here's an explanation of each column heading.

- **Context:** *What happens or what is said right before and after this passage?*
- **What?** *In 25–30 words, how can I summarize what's happening or what the author says?*
- **Who?** *What people or groups does the passage mention?*
- **Commands:** *What imperatives, both time-bound and timeless, can I find?*
- **When?** *What references to time or the timing of events in relation to each other does the passage offer?*

- **Where?** *What places are mentioned?*

- **Cause-Effect:** *Are the author's words prompted by something his readers said or did? Did one event happen as a result of another?*

- **Repetitions:** *What words, behaviors, topics, or ideas surface repeatedly?*

- **Figures of Speech:** *What does the author convey through comparisons or figurative language?*

- **Contrasts:** *What contrasting attitudes, responses, circumstances, and phraseology do I see?*

- **Classifications:** *Can I lump some of the facts I've uncovered into different categories, such as types of people or various areas of life addressed?*

- **Digging Deeper:** *What doctrinal terms, historical allusions, or obscure remarks will require extra-biblical research later on?*

I know what you're thinking. This is tedious, detailed stuff! You're right, but after you try it a few times, you will have trained your eyes to see the material. Then you won't need to use the chart on a regular basis. You'll naturally spot the repetitions, contrasts, commands, and so on.

Also be aware that not every Bible passage contains every type of factual content. But remember the maxim: If you're looking for something, you're more likely to find it! And don't worry about analyzing the facts as you record them. During the next phase of study, you'll discover truths that stem from the soil of your observation.

The key to observation is to know what to look for.

If you want to practice this observation method, use the chart while studying Matthew 4:1-11; Matthew 6:5-13; and Nehemiah 1:1-11. I'll be using these passages to illustrate kinds of questions in the next two chapters. (Your follow-through on this suggestion is not a prerequisite for understanding future chapters. Feel free to proceed with your reading if this study project isn't feasible at this time.)

OBSERVATION CHART FOR

_____

CONTEXT	WHAT	WHO
COMMANDS	WHEN	WHERE
CAUSE-EFFECT	FIGURES OF SPEECH	REPETITIONS
CONTRASTS	CLASSIFICATIONS	DIG DEEPER

FOCUSING ON MEANING

When you observe, you identify factual elements or what the passage says. When you interpret, you analyze the facts to come up with meaning. Solid interpretation requires a careful process that's satisfied with nothing less than God-intended conclusions.

Don't make the mistake of thinking interpretation is only for pastors, Bible college students, or scholars. God wrote his Word to all his people. He wouldn't inspire a Bible that only the elite can understand. Sure, we need some expert help grasping a few doctrines and obscure parts of Scripture, but most passages offer can't-miss principles if we're willing to exercise our mental muscles.

Seminary libraries teem with books that treat hermeneutics, the science of interpretation, with microscopic scrutiny. But I'm going to boil it all down into a simple four-step procedure. When you're preparing for a Bible discussion, before you consult a commentary or published curriculum, try the following suggestions.

Definition: Interpretation
Your identification of timeless truths stated in, or implied and illustrated by, passage content.

WISE WORDS

"Interpretation is the step where you pull all the facts together into a coherent explanation of their meaning. To illustrate the process, let's use the example of buying a used car. You have studied the car carefully, kicked the tires, poked under the hood, taken it for a drive, and even had a mechanic look it over. You've gathered all the facts. You conclude that it's a bad investment because the facts indicate the car is a lemon. That's interpretation—determining the meaning once all the facts are in. Interpretation is built on thorough observation."

—Hans Finzel, *Observe, Interpret, Apply*

SIMPLIFYING THE STEPS

Step 1: Prayer

The Holy Spirit who inspired Scripture also illuminates its meaning. He sheds light on passages that otherwise leave us in the dark. Jesus promised, *"But when he, the Spirit of truth, comes, he will guide you into all truth. He will not speak on his own; he will speak only what he hears, and he will tell you what is yet to come"* (John 16:13). Jesus' words may have carried special meaning for the original disciples, but the apostle Paul implied that the Holy Spirit serves as a Bible interpreter for all believers: *"No one knows the thoughts of God except the Spirit of God. We have not received the spirit of the world but the Spirit who is from God, that we may understand what God has freely given us"* (1 Corinthians 2:11, 12).

As you realize your need for illumination, remember to pray as you study a Bible passage. With a spirit of humility and dependence, ask the Lord to clarify timeless truths in the text. When you're stumped, implore him to open mental locks. Adopt the teachable spirit reflected in the psalmist's prayer: *"Open my eyes that I may see wonderful things in your law"* (Psalm 119:18).

TRY THIS!

Make this "Interpreter's Prayer" your own: *Father, as I study this passage, I acknowledge my need of your Spirit's illumination. I want to glean from your Word what you originally intended for me to receive. Nothing more . . . but nothing less! So crystallize my thinking. Show me precisely what you are saying or illustrating with all the passage elements. Don't allow my preconceived notions or personal experiences to usurp the authority of the text itself. I ask this because I want to know you better and serve you more faithfully. Amen.*

Step 2: Probes

I'd like to give you a "no-sweat" set of directions, a works-like-a-charm-every-time procedure to expedite your analysis of Scripture, but that's unrealistic. The mental gymnastics are too complicated for a patented approach. Besides, the calibration in every human brain is set differently. But there's one thing I can say with assurance: *Interpreting God's Word requires the cultivation of curiosity.* As you develop that curiosity, your mind will begin to ask a rapid-fire barrage of questions about the passage. Drop the welcome mat to any inquiries within your mind that seek the meaning of biblical information.

Remember: God's truth is objective reality. The process of probing for meaning doesn't "create" truth in any sense. Instead, it's a way to discover what God says through the facts of the text. So after you've prayed for illumination, pry open the passage with probes of all kinds. Since the same series of questions won't unlock every Bible passage, the best way to explain this investigative process is to demonstrate it.

What follows are two observations I've hoisted from a historical narrative. You'll see the questions that percolate in my mind as I seek to determine truth, then the interpretive conclusion or principle I formulate. Perhaps a peek at my probes will serve as a catalyst to your own thinking. Matthew 4:1-11 describes Jesus' bout with Satan preceding the launch of his public ministry.

Matthew 4:1-11

Observation: In response to all three temptations, Jesus quoted Scripture. He started each rebuttal with the words, "It is written."

Probes: What's the significance of this repetition? What was the effect of Jesus' quotations on Satan? How does the content of the Old Testament verses Jesus used relate to the content of a temptation? What is God saying to the contemporary reader about succeeding in spiritual warfare?

Observation: Satan tempted Jesus three times, not just once. When Jesus rebuffed the first and second temptations, Satan retaliated with a different lure.

Probes: So what? Is this fact important? Why or why not? What does the number of temptations reveal about Satan? Does the number suggest anything about the spiritual warfare I face?

The probing questions you'll ask yourself are your prayerful analysis of what a passage says. You ponder the importance of context, the implications of consequences experienced by characters, the significance of repetitions, and so on.

Your effort to interpret a passage doesn't negate the need for expert help. Discerning meaning often requires background knowledge not contained in a verse or passage. In 1 Timothy 1:19, 20, Paul "handed over to Satan" two men. We can't discover what he meant by following the "probes" step. Nor can we fully appreciate the meaning of "justification" in Romans 5:1 apart from someone's explanation of that doctrine. Also, not every truth requires analysis to find. Many are directly stated. Titus 1:2 declares that God does not lie. In Ephesians 2:8, 9 Paul asserts that we're saved by grace through faith, not by our works. These conclusions don't require the "probes" step.

Step 3: Principles

The purpose of your probing is to identify universal truths, which we'll call principles. Not all the questions you ask will result in identification of truths. You'll conclude that some of the facts you scrutinize don't contain significant meaning, and the answers to some of your questions will require extra-biblical research. But your prayerful probing of factual material should begin to spawn interpretations. The very process of posing the questions will often unveil insights that an uninquisitive mind would miss.

When a mental lightbulb comes on and you spot an insight implied by the text, summarize your conclusion in one or two sentences. Trim the fat off your thinking and refine your ideas until the point stands out with clarity, accuracy, and simplicity.

Here are principles I formulated from my observations and probes on Matthew 4:1-11. These conclusions don't require the wisdom of Solomon, but they serve to illustrate the process.

➤ *Jesus' quotation of Old Testament verses in response to each temptation demonstrates a principle about spiritual warfare: A working knowledge of God's Word is an effective defense against temptation to sin.*

➤ *That Satan tempted Jesus three times, not just once, suggests the following insight: In his attempts to derail God's purposes and defeat God's people, Satan is persistent.*

Step 4: Proofs

We can't "prove" the accuracy of an interpretation in a scientific sense. Here, proof refers to the evidence or support that bolsters the validity of the truths we find. Here are three ways to fortify our conclusions.

❶ **Passage Support**— What words or actions in the text we're studying serve as a basis for our conclusion? Does a particular statement, course of action, or repetition undergird the principle?

❷ **Support from Other Scriptures**— Does the treatment of this topic elsewhere in the Bible corroborate our conclusion? One part of Scripture will not contradict another. The broader our knowledge of the Bible, the better our ability to interpret any single passage.

❹ Extra-Biblical Support—This is when we consult published curriculum or a commentary and ask: *Does my viewpoint dovetail with expert opinion on these verses?*

The minimum I suggest doing for this "proofs" step is to determine how the facts of your passage spawned the principles you discovered. Then if you use a leader's guide or teacher's manual, you can examine it and add the author's insights to your own. Often you'll discover for yourself truths that an expert emphasizes in print, and that confirmation will excite and encourage you!

LINKING TRUTH TO LIFE

The final phase of personal Bible study is application. The goal of application is obedience to God's Word, which requires pondering how its content should affect our priorities, emotions, decisions, and relationships.

During observation and interpretation phases, we sift through God's Word. During application, God's Word sifts through us. When we try to apply the text to our lives before we lead a Bible study on it, we follow the progression Paul emphasized in 1 Timothy 4:16: "Watch your life and doctrine closely. Persevere in them, because if you do, you will save both yourself and your hearers."

Definition: Application

Identifying attitude and behavioral changes that spring logically from God's truth.

As you study a Bible passage, keep your antenna up for insights that have a bearing on your needs. Forge a link between content and situations you typically face. One way I often personalize a passage is to approach it devotionally before I plan a discussion on it. The following questions accelerate my personal application. The ideal approach is to proceed through the observation and interpretation steps first, but I've often benefited by using just these questions to explore a passage.

➤ *How does this passage increase my appreciation for God the Father, Jesus Christ, or the Holy Spirit?*

➤ *What reasons for praising the Lord does the text offer?*

➤ *What sin to avoid or forsake does the content expose?*

➤ *What positive course of action does the passage propose?*

➤ *What bearing do these verses have upon my prayer life?*

➤ *What encourages me from the passage? Why?*

➤ *What circumstances, decisions, or people come to mind as I read?*

Questions of that sort funnel truth to my heart, not just my head. When a point touches me personally, my excitement spills over during the group session because I'm convinced the passage is potent.

BRINGING IT HOME

➤ To observe a Bible passage, look for certain kinds of information.

➤ Your interpretation of Scripture requires dependence on the Holy Spirit and asking questions about what a passage says.

➤ Your application of God's Word requires an effort to identify its practical implications.

TRY THIS!

Questions that pry open your heart and reveal practical implications for you can have the same effect on other participants. Did you find reasons for praise and encouragement in the text? So can your group members! Did you spot an association between a verse and your prayer life? So can they! The most productive devotional questions will also work well during the group meeting. Find room for them in your discussion plan.

Now it's time to discover how to help your group members observe, interpret, and apply the Bible passage. In chapters 3 and 4, I'll show you how to ask discussion questions that correspond to all three phases.

Formulating Observation Questions

Questions are a crowbar for the mind. See if the following queries lift your lid.

- *Ever wonder what the speed of lightning would be if it didn't zigzag?*
- *Whatever happened to Preparations A through G?*
- *If olive oil comes from olives, where does baby oil come from?*
- *Why is the man who invests all your money called a "broker"?*
- *If ignorance is bliss, why aren't more people happy?*
- *If the #2 pencil is more popular, why is it still #2?*
- *Why do they sterilize needles for lethal injections?*
- *Do cemetery workers prefer the graveyard shift?*
- *If a book about failures doesn't sell, is it a success?*
- *Why is the word abbreviation so long?*

You can't answer all those questions satisfactorily. (I'm not sure you'd want to.) But you do want your group members to give satisfactory responses to your Bible-study questions. They will—if you ask the right kinds and word them well. This chapter and the next describe three kinds of questions that spark life-changing discussions. Chapter 5 offers guidelines for the wording of sound questions. You'll learn how to come up with your own questions or adapt and supplement those provided in published leader's guides.

In This Chapter...

- Advanced preparation of questions
- Three kinds of Bible-study questions
- Examples of observation questions

Caution

Learning the material on questioning in chapters 3–5 requires focused attention. Read these chapters when you aren't rushed or distracted. The information is clear and practical, but necessarily involves you in brief explorations of three short Bible passages. That's the only way you'll grasp the numerous examples I provide.

Before we delve into questioning, rivet this point deeply into your mind: if you want to ask original questions in your group meeting, write them in advance. Winging it with your questions deflates discussions just as surely as failing to prepare Bible content.

Wise Words

"Questioning may be the most common, widely used, and universally accepted instruction strategy. And therein lies the problem. It is much too taken for granted and too much used without insight or conscious awareness. Some ways of using questions are more effective than others. Clear, cogent, well-sequenced questions are not prepared on the spot. Discussion is an activity for which we must prepare."

—Maryellen Weimer, Improving Your Classroom Teaching

LUBRICATING YOUR BIBLE LESSONS

A man I know took his car in for an oil change. He paid the bill and then ran errands for a couple hours. He started hearing grinding noises coming from the engine. Before he arrived home, the engine locked up and stopped completely. Whoever drained the dirty oil from his car forgot to add the new oil. A lack of lubrication burned and ruined the engine. Like our cars, Bible discussions operate more efficiently when we lubricate them with OIL.

> *Observation questions*

> *Interpretation questions*

> *Life-related questions*

These types of questions correspond to the three phases of Bible study explored in chapter 2. However, here I'm substituting "life-related" for "application." (After all, "OIA" doesn't spell anything!) This approach shuttles your group members through the observe, interpret, and apply phases of Bible study. The remainder of this chapter zeroes in on observation questions. In chapter 4 you'll set your scope on interpretation and life-related questions. Digest this material, and you'll discover the joy of guiding your group members into the Word of God.

FORMULATING OBSERVATION QUESTIONS

Well-intentioned facilitators often pose analytical questions to start a

Bible study. But that's putting the proverbial cart before the horse. First, you want group members to examine what a passage says. Then their analysis is more polished and accurate. Observation questions guide participants to carefully selected facts that set the stage for interpretation. Your basis for preparing them is your own absorption of the material. You sift through the passage and separate the most important facts from the less important. Then you guide participants into the Bible to locate that information for themselves. Since the Word of God is a change agent, anytime you have them read verses during a session you've accomplished something.

TRY THIS!

Distribute blank copies of the "Observation Chart" from Chapter 2 (page 24). Explain its purpose and assign two or three columns that are pertinent to the particular passage you're studying together. Give them a few minutes to record the imperatives, repetitions, contrasts—whatever facts "open up" that passage for them. Time constraints will limit them to two or three columns. This exercise discloses key information in the text and provides a tool that more motivated participants can use for their personal Bible study.

Here's what observation questions accomplish:

- *They provide an overview of the passage. Participants spot the flow of action, key characters, advice offered, or the author's primary arguments.*
- *They reveal threads of information such as repetition of words or ideas or patterns of behavior.*
- *They inform interpretation, exposing participants to the material that spawns a timeless truth or principle for living. When you identify a truth in your preparation, you obviously base the conclusion on something that's said or something that happens in the passage. An observation question steers them to that information before you lead them to an analysis of it. The details that support a principle may reside in a single verse or may stem from a thread of information spread over several verses.*

EXAMPLES OF OBSERVATION QUESTIONS

Showing you examples will facilitate your own preparation of observation questions. I'll use three Scripture passages as the basis. If I were leading a group study of these texts, I wouldn't necessarily ask these factual questions back to back. Interpretation questions might come between them. I'm merely showing you a few questions I might ask. After each question, I'll explain why I'm posing it. Taking a peek at my thought process may help you see the value of each question.

Matthew 4:1-11

This episode describes Jesus' clash with Satan right before Jesus launched his public ministry. The verses reveal Satan's traits and tactics. Jesus demonstrates how a knowledge of Scripture helps defeat Satan.

1 Then Jesus was led by the Spirit into the desert to be tempted by the devil. 2 After fasting forty days and forty nights, he was hungry. 3 The tempter came to him and said, "If you are the Son of God, tell these stones to become bread." 4 Jesus answered, "It is written: 'Man does not live on bread alone, but on every word that comes from the mouth of God.'" 5 Then the devil took him to the holy city and had him stand on the highest point of the temple. 6 "If you are the Son of God," he said, "throw yourself down. For it is written: "'He will command his angels concerning you, and they will lift you up in their hands, so that you will not strike your foot against a stone.'" 7 Jesus answered him, "It is also written: 'Do not put the Lord your God to the test.'" 8 Again, the devil took him to a very high mountain and showed him all the kingdoms of the world and their splendor. 9 "All this I will give you," he said, "if you will bow down and worship me." 10 Jesus said to him, "Away from me, Satan! For it is written: 'Worship the Lord your God, and serve him only.'" 11 Then the devil left him, and angels came and attended him.

➤ What specific temptations did Satan fling at Jesus? I ask this very early in the study. Answering it provides a skeletal outline of the action, unveiling the organizational framework for the story.

➤ What were Jesus' circumstances immediately preceding the first temptation? In verse 2 they'll see a reference to Jesus' 40-day fast. I'm preparing the soil for an interpretation. They'll realize that Jesus was more vulnerable to this temptation—to turn stones into bread—because of his hunger. This investigation leads us to a conclusion: Satan often attacks at a person's point of greatest need or vulnerability.

➤ What did Jesus' responses to the three temptations have in common? Participants who aren't already familiar with this story will skim the verses and notice that Jesus quotes Scripture all three times. This repetition births a principle: a working knowledge of God's Word is an antidote to temptation.

Matthew 6:5-13

This passage unveils Jesus' teaching on prayer and his model prayer, which offers guidelines for the content of our prayers.

5 "And when you pray, do not be like the hypocrites, for they love to pray standing in the synagogues and on the street corners to be seen by men. I tell you the truth, they have received their reward in full. 6 But when you pray, go into your room, close the door and pray to your Father, who is unseen. Then your Father, who sees what is done in secret, will reward you. 7 And when you pray, do not keep on babbling like pagans, for they think they will be heard because of their many words. 8 Do not be like them, for your Father knows what you need before you ask him. 9 'This, then, is how you should pray: 'Our Father in heaven, hallowed be your name, 10 your kingdom come, your will be done on earth as it is in heaven. 11 Give us today our daily bread. 12 Forgive us our debts, as we also have forgiven our debtors. 13 And lead us not into temptation, but deliver us from the evil one.'"

➤ What repetitions of words or ideas can you find in verses 5-8? Jesus said "when you pray" three times in verses 5-7. Prayer is an expected, assumed practice for believers. Three times Jesus referred to God as "Father" (vv. 6, 8). This view of God motivates us to pray, for the term connotes his desire for intimacy with us and his parental concern for us. The most effective observation questions force learners to scan several verses or find multiple answers. This keeps the factual assignment from being too obvious.

➤ Summarize in your own words the requests Jesus makes in verses 10-13. Occasionally, I put an observation assignment in directive rather than the interrogative form. This assignment causes them to identify elements of Jesus' prayer. Paraphrasing the verses is a bit more challenging than merely parroting them back. Each verse or petition leads to a timeless guideline for the content of our prayers. For instance, in verse 13 Jesus advocates what I call "warfare praying" to protect us from the onslaught of temptations that threaten us.

Now That's A Good Question! **35**

Nehemiah 1:1-11

Nehemiah, a servant of the Babylonian king, received discouraging news about the Jewish remnant who had returned to Jerusalem from captivity. He's so distraught he weeps and fasts for days. Verses 5-11 record his intercession on their behalf.

1 The words of Nehemiah son of Hacaliah: In the month of Kislev in the twentieth year, while I was in the citadel of Susa, 2 Hanani, one of my brothers, came from Judah with some other men, and I questioned them about the Jewish remnant that survived the exile, and also about Jerusalem. 3 They said to me, "Those who survived the exile and are back in the province are in great trouble and disgrace. The wall of Jerusalem is broken down, and its gates have been burned with fire." 4 When I heard these things, I sat down and wept. For some days I mourned and fasted and prayed before the God of heaven. 5 Then I said: "O Lord, God of heaven, the great and awesome God, who keeps his covenant of love with those who love him and obey his commands, 6 let your ear be attentive and your eyes open to hear the prayer your servant is praying before you day and night for your servants, the people of Israel. I confess the sins we Israelites, including myself and my father's house, have committed against you. 7 We have acted very wickedly toward you. We have not obeyed the commands, decrees and laws you gave your servant Moses. 8 Remember the instruction you gave your servant Moses, saying, 'If you are unfaithful, I will scatter you among the nations, 9 but if you return to me and obey my commands, then even if your exiled people are at the farthest horizon, I will gather them from there and bring them to the place I have chosen as a dwelling for my Name.' 10 "They are your servants and your people, whom you redeemed by your great strength and your mighty hand. 11 O Lord, let your ear be attentive to the prayer of this your servant and to the prayer of your servants who delight in revering your name. Give your servant success today by granting him favor in the presence of this man." I was cupbearer to the king.

➤ How did Nehemiah discover the plight of the Jews in Jerusalem? They'll notice that Nehemiah questioned his visitors about the Jews. This fact spawns a principle: inquisitiveness is integral to intercession. We can pray more specifically and intelligently for people when we take the initiative to discover their needs.

➤ What attributes of God did Nehemiah cite in his prayer? Verse 5 indicates that the Lord is a great, awesome, loving, and promise-keeping God. Next, pose an interpretation question to help participants articulate this principle: intercession is fueled by an awareness of God's attributes. Focusing on him at the start of our prayers reminds us that he is capable and concerned enough to intervene and address our burdens.

➤ What words in verses 4-11 reveal Nehemiah's humility? To determine that Nehemiah was humble requires analysis of what he did and said. The text doesn't say he was humble. Normally my group analyzes a passage only after examining the facts on which the interpretation is based. But here I reverse the process. I state that he's humble, and ask them to find the evidence for it. His weeping and fasting (v. 4), plus his confession of sin (vv. 6, 7) show his contrition. Following this observation question we'll conclude that humility and a soft heart are prerequisites for the ministry of intercession.

SEQUENCING OF QUESTIONS

I'll explore interpretation and life-related questions in the next chapter. But here I'll illustrate a sequence to follow in covering a principle. First I pose an observation question, then an interpretive one rooted in those facts, and then I move directly to a life-related question on that particular verse or truth. I don't necessarily ask all the observation questions before moving to the interpretation probes. I move through the three types of questions while camping out on a single point, and then I may ask another observation question on a different section of the passage. Here's an example of three consecutive questions that I ask about Nehemiah 1.

1 **Observation:** How did Nehemiah discover the plight of the Jews?

2 **Interpretation:** What prerequisite for effective intercession does his inquiry illustrate?

3 **Life-Related:** In what ways can we stay informed concerning the needs of people in this group or in our church?

Now That's A Good Question! **37**

DISCUSSION DISCLAIMER

Questions aren't the only way to review factual content. If you're pressed for time in your group meeting, save several minutes by summarizing the factual material on which a principle is based and just ask an interpretation question. Instead of asking, "What were the three temptations Satan flung at Jesus?" recap for them the temptations and go straight to an interpretation question: "What do these particular lures tell us about Satan's tactics?"

CAUTION!

You want group members to absorb basic facts, but avoid excessive reliance on observation questions. Be sure to reserve ample time for the more important interpretation and life-related questions.

CHECK THIS OUT!

Give group members time to read the Bible passage during your meeting before you start asking questions. If you're studying a chapter or less, let them skim the entire passage before you pose questions on specific verses. This enables them to see the larger context before they examine its parts. For longer texts, have them read just the set of verses on which a question is based before you ask it.

Another example. This question is too obvious: "How many temptations did Jesus face?" Just ask an interpretive question rooted in the fact that he faced three temptations, not one. "What do the number of temptations tell us about Satan?" The observation phase is essential, but use common sense and let the passage dictate how you cover the material.

YOUR TURN!

No one learns how to cook, swim, or change a flat tire solely by reading a how-to book. To acquire a skill requires putting into practice what you read. It's the familiar "learning by doing" approach. That's true for preparing Bible-study questions too. Here's your chance to practice what you have read on the previous pages.

Read Philippians 1:1-11 carefully. Paul thanks the Philippians for a monetary gift they'd sent him. He expresses his affection and prays for them. Paul founded the church on his first missionary journey, so their relationship goes way back. A possible title for this passage is *How Does Fellowship Show?* The bond between Paul and the Philippians teems with application for us. Read verses 1 through 11, then develop two observation questions to ask during a group study of these verses.

Next I'll show you how to prepare even more important interpretation and life-related questions.

BRINGING IT HOME

➤ *Asking original Bible-study questions involves advanced preparation.*

➤ *Lubricate lessons with O-I-L: a blend of observation, interpretation, and life-related questions.*

➤ *Observation questions enable group members to absorb what a passage says before they try to interpret it.*

➤ *When you're pushed for time, just state the facts and only ask interpretation questions that spring from them.*

TEAM-BUILDING FUN!

Distribute name tags or note cards. Tell everyone to write his first name vertically on the tag or card. Instruct each person to use each letter of his name as the first letter of a single word that tells something about his personality, hobbies, past experiences—you name it! P could stand for a recent "promotion." E could start the word "exercise" and refer to a gym membership, and so on. Then everyone can explain his acrostic to the group. (If you teach a large class, form groups of four-to-six persons for this activity.)

Asking Interpretation & Life-Related Questions

Through our churches we work long and hard to communicate the gospel to a needy world. But it seems we aren't as effective when communicating within our own ranks. Someone culled the following announcements from various church bulletins and newsletters. Notice how an inadvertent placement or omission of words permits an errant interpretation.

✦ *During the absence of our pastor, we enjoyed the rare privilege of hearing a good sermon when J. F. Stubbs supplied our pulpit.*

✦ *Reverend Merriwether spoke briefly, much to the delight of the audience.*

✦ *For those of you who have children and don't know it, we have a nursery downstairs.*

✦ *The pastor will preach his farewell message, after which the choir will sing, "Break Forth into Joy."*

✦ *Don't let worry kill you off; let the church help.*

✦ *The ladies of the church have cast off clothing of every kind, and they can be seen in the church basement Friday afternoon.*

✦ *This afternoon there will be a meeting in the south and north ends of the church. Children will be baptized at both ends.*

✦ *Remember in prayer the many who are sick of our church and community.*

✦ *The cost for attending the "Fasting and Prayer" conference includes meals.*

+ *Next Thursday will be tryouts for the choir. They need all the help they can get.*

+ *The peacemaking meeting scheduled for today has been canceled due to a conflict.*

+ *Sermon title: "The Role of Women in the Church." Closing hymn: "Rise up, O Men of God!"*

Transferring a message from one person's mind to another's is sometimes a precarious process. Incorrectly interpreting someone else's words can be humorous, but when it comes to Bible study and teaching, accurate interpretation is essential. This chapter shows you how to assist group members in their search for meaning and how to shuttle them toward application of the truths they discover.

FORMULATING INTERPRETATION QUESTIONS

In Chapter 2 I defined interpretation as the *identification of timeless truths stated, implied, or illustrated by passage content.* I presented a simple, step-by-step procedure to expedite your analysis of facts. When it comes to your group Bible discussions, interpretation questions are those that enable learners to discern meaning couched in passage facts.

As a Bible-discussion leader, you're a guide to learning. You've dug into the text and uncovered treasure in the form of truth. Now it's your privilege to lead others on an expedition into God's Word. You could just dole out the riches you found by lecturing, but you're too sharp to take that route. You realize people are more likely to cherish and keep nuggets of truth when they do their own digging.

"Good questions have a purpose. Questions should be written to accomplish one of the three steps of the inductive method (observation, interpretation, application), and they should in some way relate to the topic and the theme for the Bible passage."

— Jim Wilhoit and Leland Ryken,
Effective Bible Teaching

That's where interpretation questions enter the picture. Posing sound, analytical questions is like handing learners picks and shovels. Your queries equip them to uncover insights located just beneath the surface.

Take a look at the following checklist for interpretation questions. These guidelines will help you evaluate each probe you prepare. A good analytical question will muster a yes on each of these queries.

✔ Can participants point to specific passage elements to support their answers? (Meaning stems from what the passage says, not speculation about the material.)

✔ Does my question require them to explain the meaning implied or illustrated by the facts? (If participants come up with an answer just by reiterating what the text says, it's an observation question, not an interpretive one.)

✔ Can group members answer correctly by sticking to the information provided in this Bible passage? (Don't ask questions requiring historical background or doctrinal discernment that's outside the scope of the lesson. If understanding your text requires that sort of material, briefly lecture on it.)

✔ Is the answer to this question a significant truth offered by the passage? (In view of time limitations and group characteristics, covering every truth in your Bible passage isn't always realistic. Shoot for principles that best correlate with the passage's main theme and have the greatest application potential.)

Caution

Don't allow the wording of interpretation questions to put the spotlight on personal opinion rather than the Bible text. Avoid questions such as, "What does this verse mean to you?" This question causes participants to turn inward and promotes excessive subjectivity rather than objective investigation of a passage.

Pondering that checklist will help you think through the purpose and potential of each probe you're considering and will enable you to weed out questions that might be ineffective. With these guidelines you should be well equipped for developing solid interpretation questions.

SAMPLE INTERPRETATION QUESTIONS

What follows are a few interpretation questions I've used during a group study of three passages. I employed the same passages in chapter 3 to illustrate observation questions. If it's been a while since you've read chapter 3, go back and skim Matthew 4:1-11; Matthew 6:5-13; and Nehemiah 1:1-11. The texts of these Bible passages are included in chapter 3.

Before formulating an interpretation question, you must identify a truth that you want participants to find. Before I show you my questions, I provide the principle I'm wanting group members to see and the factual support for that principle. I'm hoping that this material will jumpstart your thinking and make it easier for you to write your own interpretation questions.

INTERPRETATION QUESTION 1 — Matthew 4:1-11

➤ **Principle:** In his attempts to derail God's purposes and defeat God's people, Satan is persistent.

➤ **Factual Support:** Satan tempted Jesus three times, not just once. Despite being rebuffed after the first two temptations, Satan tried yet again.

➤ **Interpretation Question:** What does the number of temptations tell us about Satan?

INTERPRETATION QUESTION 2

➤ **Principle:** A working knowledge of God's Word can help us defeat temptation.

➤ **Factual Support:** In response to all three temptations, Jesus said, "It is written," and then proceeded to quote from the Old Testament. The content of the verses he recited corresponded to the nature of each temptation.

➤ **Interpretation question:** What insight about handling temptation did Jesus model for us?

INTERPRETATION QUESTION I — Matthew 6:5-13

➤ **Principle:** Proper motives for praying include a promised reward and God's personal concern for his people.

➤ **Factual support:** Jesus stated that God will repay those who pray in secret (v. 6). He referred to God as "Father" in verses 6 and 8 and said that God is aware of our needs (v. 8).

➤ **Interpretation question:** Examine verses 5-8. What commendable motives for praying can you find?

INTERPRETATION QUESTION 2

➤ **Principle:** Guidelines for the content of our prayers include starting with a focus on God, interceding for what's on God's heart, petition for personal needs, confession of sin, and prayer for protection against temptation and Satan.

➤ **Factual support:** Each of these conclusions stem from a separate verse in verses 9-13. Analysis of what Jesus says in each verse leads to a timeless guideline for our praying.

➤ **Interpretation question:** Analyze Jesus' words in verses 9-13. What guidelines for the content of our prayers can you find?

Special Note: Occasionally a single interpretation question uncovers multiple principles. You can view each prayer guideline in verses 9-13 as a separate principle.

INTERPRETATION QUESTION I — Nehemiah I:I-II

➤ **Principle:** Humility and a soft heart are prerequisites for consistent intercession.

➤ **Factual support:** Nehemiah wept, mourned, and fasted when he heard the plight of the Jews in Jerusalem (vv. 3, 4). He identified with the sins of Israel that had led to the Babylonian captivity, for he said, "I confess the sins we . . . have committed" (v. 6) and "we have acted very wickedly toward you" (v. 7).

➤ **Interpretation question:** In verses 4-7, what traits are implied by Nehemiah's actions and words? (Pause for responses). Why are these qualities essential to the ministry of intercession?

INTERPRETATION QUESTION 2

➤ **Principle:** A spirit of inquisitiveness, taking the initiative to discover others' needs, facilitates a ministry of intercession.

➤ **Factual support:** When an entourage from Jerusalem visited Nehemiah in Babylonia, he questioned them concerning the Jews who escaped captivity and about Jerusalem (v. 2).

➤ **Interpretation question:** What insight about intercession can we glean from verse 2?

PREPARING LIFE-RELATED QUESTIONS

A Bible discussion isn't complete until you add life-related questions that prompt participants to connect truths to their lives. Even if it means covering less Bible content, time for application questions is essential. Less is sometimes more. A greater quantity of content covered doesn't necessarily mean that a greater quantity of content has been learned. What matters is how much content participants process, not how much you expose them to.

In chapter 2 I provided a series of questions to enhance your devotions and help you personalize a passage before you teach it. In this section, I'll illustrate questions to ask group members so they can personalize the content.

> **"Interpretation without application is abortion of the Word of God."**
> **— Howard Hendricks**

Application refers to participants' response to Scripture, but the group meeting isn't usually the setting where obedience occurs. After folks disperse, that's when they choose to heed or ignore the Spirit's leading. When the Holy Spirit points out a needed change, the contexts for obedience include the home, schools, and the marketplace.

Remember: What matters is how much content participants process, not how much you expose them to.

That's why "teaching for application" doesn't refer to the attitude or behavioral change itself. Instead, it's the guided process of helping group members identify follow-through possibilities. You can't guarantee that anyone will apply or obey God's Word. But you can make sure people leave with life implications percolating in their minds. Your job is to help them "see" applications.

A WAY OF THINKING

Application is a mind-set that isn't satisfied with what a text says or means. It's a way of thinking that constantly asks, "So what?" in response to content. To help sensitize me to a Bible study's implications for my learners, I ponder the questions that follow. These aren't questions I ask the group, but thinking about them increases the likelihood that I'll spend meeting time on application. It's my way of keeping one eye on the Bible passage and the other eye on my learners' needs and schedules.

- *What relationship does this principle have to my group members?*
- *What roles, relationships, and responsibilities serve as contexts for their application of this lesson?*
- *In view of my group members' life situations, what hindrances to applications will they likely face?*
- *What kind of assistance or support system could help them apply this lesson?*
- *If participants heed this lesson, what positive effect will it have on their attitudes? Their decisions? Their schedules?*
- *If people ignore the passage's implication for their lives, what negative consequences will they experience?*
- *When the group meets, how can I illustrate the benefits of obeying this passage or the painful outcome of ignoring it?*

TYPES OF LIFE-RELATED QUESTIONS

Now let's examine three types of life-related questions.

1 Ask for anecdotes.

Plan questions that draw out personal examples from participants. Ask them to provide scenarios for application. Let their experiences convey the benefits of obeying truth or the consequences of ignoring it. Personal questions catapult people from the comprehension level to the changed-life level of learning. Group members are compelled to think about the transfer of truth to life. Before each example, I reiterate the principle on which it's based.

Matthew 4:1-11 illustrates this principle of spiritual warfare: a working knowledge of Scripture is an effective antidote to temptation.

> ➤ **Life-related question:** Who can illustrate the power of God's Word to sustain or assist you during bouts of spiritual warfare?

Matthew 6:5-13 conveys this truth: Our heavenly Father rewards our praying (v. 6).

> ➤ **Life-related question:** Who can illustrate a benefit or answer you've received in response to prayer?

Nehemiah 1:8, 9 demonstrates that the promises God has made motivate intercession.

> ➤ **Life-related question:** When has awareness of a biblical promise prompted you to pray for someone?

Ask for anecdotes only after you've already guided the group through the observation and interpretation phases of Bible study. God's truth, not personal experience, is the focal point of the discussion. The truth you're seeking to illustrate always deserves top billing. Yet slice-of-life stories solidify God's truth in learners' minds and jog their thinking about application.

✔ **CHECK THIS OUT!**

"Asking for anecdotes" works better when group members have been Christians for a few years. They have more experience in relation to the principles you discuss, so it's easier to think of apt illustrations. If your group consists of new believers, ask fewer questions of this type. Instead, share more stories from your own spiritual pilgrimage. Even when participants are mature believers, this kind of question often requires transparency, so don't direct them to individuals. Leave them open-ended so responses are voluntary.

2 Probe for possibilities.

The next type of life-related question is the one you'll rely on most often. Discuss realistic ways to respond to God's truth. Ask group members to imagine what application of the principle will look like. When application ideas saturate their minds, the Holy Spirit has fuel with which to work after the group disperses.

Matthew 4:1-11 reveals that Satan is persistent. My group discussed the need for our own persistence in our battle against temptation.

> ➤ **Life-related question:** In what specific ways should our persistence show?

Matthew 6:7 suggests this principle: to avoid meaningless repetition and rote-level prayers, we should engage our minds when we pray.

> ➤ **Life-related question:** What can we do to engage our minds more when we pray?

Nehemiah 1:1-11 illustrates personal qualities essential to intercession and offers motivations to pray for others.

> ➤ **Life-related question:** How can we keep "I'll pray for you" from becoming another religious cliché?

Wise Words

Charles Spurgeon, a prolific pastor of the nineteenth century, knew Bible truths eclipse illustrations in importance. Yet he realized that folks are more likely to remember and to obey a truth that's illustrated. What he told aspiring preachers also pertains to discussion facilitators: *"Examples are more powerful than precepts."* (Lectures to My Students)

3 Rhetorical questions

Occasionally a life-related question is so personal that you don't ask for oral responses. It's a penetrating probe that spurs group members to search their hearts or identify concrete responses to truths. A rhetorical question usually comes near the close of a Bible study. You wouldn't employ a rhetorical question in every session. When you do, pause after each question to give them time to ponder it. The following examples will show their usefulness.

Matthew 4:1-11

> ➤ What temptation plagues you most?

> ➤ What insight from this passage is most helpful in your battle against this particular temptation?

> ➤ What can you do differently to increase the odds of succeeding against this temptation?

Matthew 6:5-13

> ➤ Jesus advocated praying in secret. What place and time of day can you reserve for prayer that will allow you to be unhurried and free of distractions?

Nehemiah 1:1-11

➤ Think of a person or group whose current needs should prompt your intercession. To what extent are you already interceding for this person or group?

➤ Is the Holy Spirit nudging you to increase your ministry of intercession for this need?

ACKNOWLEDGING LIMITATIONS

Previously I defined "teaching for application" as the process of guiding a group to identify follow-through possibilities. You set the stage for a lesson response, but your group members are the performers. They're responsible before God to reform their relationships, reverse sinful patterns, and meet needs around them as dictated by the Bible passage.

Sometimes group members are so close-knit that they can share responses to such questions with each other. But err on the side of caution and allow them to deal privately with the Lord when necessary.

You can reserve group time to discuss a truth's implications. You can testify to the power of the passage in your own life. You can help people picture the difference a principle would make if they incorporated it into their daily routines. You can ask them for anecdotes that disclose the benefits of obeying and the consequences of neglecting God's Word. You can probe for possible responses that fit the needs and maturity levels of participants. But you cannot apply God's Word for anyone but yourself. A learner's heart is either fertile soil that welcomes the seed of Scripture or rocky ground too callous for the seed to penetrate.

There's a logical reaction to realizing your limitations: pray for your group members. When you intercede for them, you acknowledge dependence on the Holy Spirit. You're admitting that transferring truth from the head to the heart is a divine rather than human endeavor. You're asking God to accomplish what no amount of teaching excellence can: to prick their consciences, alter their attitudes, and bend their wills in the direction of biblical standards. This principle of relying on God for life change in learners is illustrated in the words of W. E.

Sangster: *"God's work, apart from prayer, produces clever ineffectiveness"* (Preaching with Power).

Pray for your group members. When you intercede for them, you acknowledge dependence on the Holy Spirit.

YOUR TURN!

In chapter 3, I encouraged you to write a couple observation questions on Philippians 1:1-11. Paul's relationship with the Philippians demonstrates timeless expressions of fellowship. Read the verses again (see chapter 3), and identify two insights about fellowship you would cover in a group Bible study. Then write one or more interpretation and life-related questions for a group discussion of the passage.

PRAYER FOR APPLICATION

Father, I'm responsible to strive for life change in my Bible discussions. Yet I'm aware of my limitations. Only you can cause a person to loathe sin. Only you can instill joy in a heart that's hurting. Only you can reconcile family members who haven't spoken to each other in years. Only you can mold a person's will until he wants to obey your Word. So if life change is going to occur among the members of my group, you must soften their hearts. I'll do my part and commit group time to discuss application, but I'm ultimately dependent on you. In the name of the one who prayed for the people he taught, amen.

> ➤ *Interpretation questions require group members to analyze passage information, not merely restate it.*

> ➤ *Identify specific truths in a passage before writing interpretation questions.*

> ➤ *Help participants connect Bible truth to life by asking life-related questions.*

> ➤ *Ask for slice-of-life illustrations of truths, brainstorm for follow-through ideas, and pose extremely personal questions rhetorically.*

> ➤ *Since your group members are ultimately responsible for applying Bible truths, pray for them.*

TRY THIS TEAMWORK IDEA!

Distribute blank name tags. Instruct participants to write or print their names in the shape of something that describes them: a symbol that captures a trait, hobby, or current circumstance. Provide examples as a catalyst to their thinking. A basketball fan could put his name in the form of a circle. Someone facing an important decision or uncertainty about the future could arrange the letters in the form of a question mark. Then let everyone display and explain his or her creation. Others can ask about the experience or sphere of interest captured in the design.

The next chapter puts the spotlight on guidelines for the wording of questions. You'll discover common mistakes discussion leaders make when they pose questions.

Identifying Guidelines for Effective Questions

Drivers were asked to explain the cause of their accidents in as few words as possible. Here are some of the more unusual responses:

In This Chapter...

Effective Bible study questions are:

- Clear
- Accurate
- Sensitive
- Thought-provoking

+ *Coming home I drove into the wrong house and collided with a tree I don't have.*

+ *I collided with a stationary car going the other way.*

+ *The telephone pole was rapidly approaching. I was attempting to swerve out of its way when it struck my front end.*

+ *A pedestrian hit me and went under my car.*

+ *The guy was all over the road. I had to swerve a number of times before I finally hit him.*

+ *I had been driving for forty years when I fell asleep at the wheel and had an accident.*

+ *My car was legally parked as it backed into the other vehicle.*

+ *I was on my way to the doctor with rear-end trouble when my universal joint gave way, causing me to have an accident.*

Apparently, their accidents impaired their ability to think clearly! This sampling of fuzzy communication massages the funny bone, but ambiguity is the last word that should describe your leadership of Bible studies. Precise language is a must, especially when you're posing questions.

In the previous two chapters I discussed three kinds of Bible-study questions: observation, interpretation, and life-related. Now let's shift the spotlight to how you word those questions. The quality of your group members' responses, or whether they respond at all, depends on the language in your questions.

It's important for you to know how to write original questions for your Bible discussions. But even if you rely on published leader's guides, this chapter will enable you to separate the good questions from the mediocre ones or to adapt the material for your particular group. Just because it's in print doesn't mean every question provided for you is sound.

WiSe Words

"Do not tell what you can ask."

— Jane Vella, *Learning to Listen, Learning to Teach*

DON'T ASK THESE QUESTIONS!

Before discussing positive criteria, I want to show you some poor questions that represent many common mistakes that I've seen Bible-study leaders make. These are questions you should not ask during a group Bible discussion. Though some of the questions are worse than others, each question breaks at least one of the wording guidelines I'll cover later.

You're in a group that's studying Matthew 4:1-11. Imagine you're hearing each question precisely as it's shown here. The passage theme is "winning at warfare." This episode on the temptations of Jesus reveals Satan's traits and tactics. Jesus demonstrates how a working knowledge of Scripture serves as an antidote to temptation. Take a moment to skim the narrative again. (See chapter 3.)

To engage your mind as you proceed through the list, jot down a phrase in the space provided that critiques each question. Tell why it's a poor choice.

What about the fact that Satan quoted Scripture during his confrontation of Jesus?	
Looking at the devil in action tempting Jesus in the wilderness, what specific qualities and strategies of spiritual warfare that he will also use against us does he demonstrate?	

What happened right before the first temptation, and what does this timing tell us about Satan?	
When the devil left, angels ministered to Jesus (v. 11). How do you think the angels ministered to him in this situation?	
Jesus fasted for forty days and nights. What are some other occasions in the Bible when forty-days are mentioned?	
What does verse 11 mean to you?	
Marge, you've been a believer for a few years. Can you tell us how you've experienced Satan's persistence in his warfare against you?	
What other names does the Bible give for the devil?	
What does it say in verse 9?	
Did Satan recognize Jesus' true identity?	
Don't you think the timing of Satan's attack on Jesus was significant?	
In verse 5, why is Jerusalem called a "holy" city?	

The problems with the previous examples will become clearer as I discuss the following guidelines. As you read each guideline, refer back to these ineffective questions and determine which guideline each one breaks.

CLEAR

The following question was spotted on a graffiti wall at St. John's University in Minnesota:

Jesus said to them, "Who do you say that I am?"

And they replied, "You are the eschatological manifestation of the ground of our being, the kerygma in which we find the ultimate meaning of our interpersonal relationships."

And Jesus said, "What?" (Jospeh Bayly, I Love Sunday School)

This imaginary dialogue reminds me of Jesus' habit of putting the bread of life on the lowest shelf, where anyone could reach it. Neither high-falutin' vocabulary nor abstract oratory impresses him—or your group members! Plain, easy-to-grasp English is the first feature of questions that pry open the human mind.

Put yourself in the shoes of your group members. Will they understand the vocabulary in your questions? Does your wording presume too much biblical or theological knowledge on their part? Can you insert a shorter word for the long one? Inspect questions for ambiguity. Recite questions aloud. Test them on your spouse or a friend to see if the intent is clear. Be on the lookout for the following foes of clarity.

Caution

Perhaps it's hard for you to believe that anyone would ask some of those bad questions. Yet I've heard well educated, gifted teachers pose questions similar to all of these. It usually happens when a discussion leader poses questions on the spot without preparing in advance. Lack of forethought increases the likelihood of poor questions.

"What About" Questions

One type of question that always drops a dark veil over group members' thinking begins with the words, "What about…?" It's a common way to launch a question in casual conversations. (What about the prayer request you mentioned last week?) But never allow "what about" to trespass into the domain of Bible-study questions. When participants hear a "what about" question, they shrug their shoulders and think, *Well, what about it?*

Run-Together Questions

Rein in the impulse to fling back-to-back questions at the group without waiting for a reply to the first one. One question at a time! I can't think of a valid exception to this rule. Either the participants will be confused about which question to answer first, or they will forget the first question by the time you finish the second one.

Long-Winded Questions

Another nemesis of clarity is the *long-winded question*. A good discussion facilitator trims the fat off an overweight question until it is lean enough to appear in a diet food commercial. Keep questions as short as possible.

A sure-fire way to prune the clutter from questions is to precede them with introductory remarks. Facts you stuff within the probe itself are more easily assimilated by learners when you put them in statements. Here's another question that's too long and cumbersome:

Memo

When you pose detailed questions about specific words or phrases in a Bible verse, realize that some group members may use a different translation than you. In Ephesians 4:11, 12, the role of church leaders is "equipping" in the New American Standard Bible, to "prepare" in the New International Version, and "perfecting" in the King James Version. Ignoring subtle variations among translations can confuse participants. Either glance at several translations while you prepare, or ask group members to give you their translation of key words that the questions address.

In light of the way Jesus responded to each of the three temptations by saying, "It is written," what principle about succeeding in spiritual warfare can we learn from him?

Instead, put the necessary facts into statements. Then use a shorter, easier-to-grasp question:

Look again at the verses recording Jesus' response to each temptation. On each occasion he employed the phrase, "It is written." What insight about handling temptation did he model for us?

ACCURATE

When it comes to Bible study, what group members conclude about a passage should match its God-intended meaning. I've encountered three adversaries to accuracy that crop up in the wording of discussion questions.

Speculative Questions

As a discussion facilitator, you're a guide who leads others on safaris into the biblical text. But when a speculative question slips into the group interaction, you may get lost in a maze of misinterpretation or meaningless mumbo-jumbo. A speculative question seeks information not disclosed in the Bible passage and tries to satisfy curiosity about a fact God figured we didn't need to know. It also promotes conjecture about the Bible rather than investigation and analysis of it.

You risk inaccuracies when your queries...

foster speculation about the text

encourage exploration of irrelevant material

shift the focus of authority from God's Word to participants' opinions

Here are additional questions I would not ask in a study of Matthew 4:1-11. No matter how long participants pore over the verses, they won't find an answer.

➡ *Jesus' baptism at the hands of John the Baptist preceded this temptation narrative (Matthew 3:13-17). How much time do you think elapsed between the baptism and Jesus' excursion into the wilderness?*

➡ *If Jesus had listened to Satan and jumped off the pinnacle of the temple, what do you think would have happened?*

➡ *The devil promised Jesus all the kingdoms of the world (vv. 8, 9). Would that promise have been fulfilled if Jesus had worshiped Satan?*

Irrelevant Questions

This type of question "majors on minors." It dissects a word, phrase, or name in a verse without consideration of its larger context. Or it focuses on details that are relatively insignificant in view of the passage's main theme.

Aiming for accuracy in a discussion isn't only a matter of avoiding speculation and outright error. It's also sticking to the overarching theme of a text and covering just those facts and truths that develop your subject slant. When less significant passage data steals the spotlight, discussion becomes a game of "trivial pursuit."

Now let's turn to the theme of Matthew 4:1-11. By examining Jesus' bout with Satan, we gain insights to help us experience victory in spiritual warfare. Matthew weaves two threads of thought through the fabric of these verses. He illustrates battle strategies and characteristics of Satan, our archenemy. Through the example of Jesus, he shows us the value of Scripture as a defense against temptation. All study questions tossed out to the group should reinforce the primary theme and lead to discovery, analysis, and application of the two specific subject slants.

Questions that Usurp Biblical Authority

Another way to encourage an inaccurate interpretation of a Bible passage is to transfer the authority from God's Word to the group members. You'd never do this intentionally, but it often happens when a group leader is inexperienced or poorly prepared. A question such as, "What does the verse mean to you?" encourages too much subjectivity and shifts the focus away from the text. It encourages people to "create meaning" rather than analyze the material.

SENSITIVE

When is a question sensitive? When you make personal responses voluntary and when you're realistic about participants' ability to answer.

Compulsory Personal Questions

Sure, you want group members to reinforce truths with anecdotes. You want them to reveal needs exposed by God's Word so your group can pray specifically for one another. In chapter 1 I stated that transparency is a vital sign of a healthy group. In chapter 4 I emphasized that soliciting illustrations can enhance a lesson's application. Go ahead and ask for examples of someone applying a truth or the consequences of neglecting it. Just don't drop a personal question in the lap of an unsuspecting participant.

Rather than asking an individual to illustrate Satan's persistence, pose the question so responses are voluntary: "Who can illustrate Satan's persistence from your experience as a Christian?" The question still calls for transparency, but now a group member's response is a matter of choice.

Unrealistic Questions

Keeping questions realistic is as important as keeping personal inquiries voluntary. Some study leaders tend to reel off questions that expect more than the average participant can deliver. Don't ask for background or cross-reference information that a typical group member won't know.

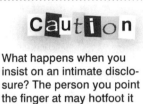

Caution

What happens when you insist on an intimate disclosure? The person you point the finger at may hotfoot it home and never return!

Other questions to avoid are those that can't be answered by direct observation or interpretation of the text.

TRY THIS!

If you know that a group member has a personal story or history that illustrates or reinforces a passage, call this person before the meeting. Ask if he or she is comfortable sharing the anecdote with others. If so, ask for this contribution at the appropriate spot in the Bible study.

➼ What Old Testament book did Jesus quote to refute Satan?

➼ What other New Testament passages offer insights on Satan and spiritual warfare?

➼ Since Jesus was divine, how was it even possible for the devil's suggestions to "tempt" him? Wasn't he above temptation?

When background or cross-reference material sheds light on your passage, take a moment to share it. Just don't expect a group member to know it.

THOUGHT-PROVOKING

Let's assume your questions are clear. Let's also assume your queries aim for accuracy by sticking to the biblical text and exalting its authority. Let's even assume their wording reveals sensitivity to group members. That's still not enough. What you ask must also stimulate thought. Unless your probes spark thought, you'll extinguish learners' enthusiasm.

Questions that drench motivation:

> ➤ *call for a yes/no response*

> ➤ *fetch effortless, obvious answers*

> ➤ *elicit agreement with our predeter-mined opinions*

Yes/No Questions

Omit questions that begin with *Do, Did, Was, Were, Is, Are*—anything that calls for a mere yes or no response. Here are two yes/no questions, along with suggested revisions.

> ➤ Did God the Father show sensitivity to the Son after this skirmish with Satan? (*Revision: Following this skirmish with Satan, how did God the Father show sensitivity to the Son?*)

> ➤ Have you ever overcome a temptation by recalling a verse or truth from Scripture? (*Revision: Who can illustrate how a knowledge of God's Word has come to your rescue during spiritual warfare?*)

Obvious Questions

A second way to douse the fires of learner participation is to rattle off questions in search of obvious information. If their eyelids get stuck at half-mast when you're firing questions, maybe you're asking group members to investigate what's already apparent. Who wants to respond when the answer is clear to everyone? Such questions merely require participants to parrot back a phrase from a single verse. These questions call for obvious answers:

> ➤ *Where did this clash between Satan and Jesus occur?*

> ➤ *How long had Jesus fasted before Satan appeared?*

> ➤ *What did the angels begin to do when they appeared in verse 11?*

Observation assignments are more challenging when they require group members to read two or more verses or come up with multiple answers. Note these examples:

➤ What were the three temptations thrust upon Jesus?

➤ What do Jesus' responses to the three temptations have in common?

Leading Questions

A third way to insult rather than incite participants' intellect is to cast "leading" questions in their direction.

Most leading questions call for a yes or no response, with a negative hitchhiking on the first word. Phrases such as "Don't you think . . ." or "Isn't . . ." are typical. (Isn't the fact that Satan tempted Jesus three times, not once, revealing?)

Definition: Leading Question

INCITE PARTICIPANTS' INTELLECT BY AVOIDING "LEADING" QUESTIONS

A leading question sags under the weight of your personal opinion or preconceived notions. How you formulate such a question actually reveals the answer you prefer to receive. Instead of encouraging people to think about a point in the text, you're asking others whether or not they agree with you.

Your Turn!

To apply these guidelines, go back to the observation, interpretation, and life-related questions you wrote on Philippians 1:1-11, as instructed, near the close of chapters 3 and 4. Evaluate your wording and see if you can improve on them.

Pleasant Experience: Give each participant a 3" x 5" card. Have each person describe on the card a pleasant experience from recent months—something the other group members aren't likely to know. Collect the cards, scramble them, and have every participant pick a card. When everyone has received a card other than his own, instruct people to find the person whose experience is recorded on the card. Then everyone can share with the whole group the pleasant experience.

BRINGING IT HOME

➤ Ask questions that are clear and simple.

➤ Be sure your questions aren't speculative, irrelevant, or encourage excessive subjectivity.

➤ Avoid compulsory personal questions and probes that require background knowledge.

➤ Avoid questions that call for merely a yes/no response, fetch obvious answers, and elicit agreement with your predetermined opinions.

In the next chapter I'll explain how to put your questions and notes in a logical sequence. You'll learn how to launch a Bible study and identify the parts of a sound discussion plan.

Organizing Your Discussion Plan

To launch his Bible study on Matthew 4:1-11, Tony distributed 3" x 5" cards. He instructed group members to write a few words completing this sentence: *"Temptation is _____ ."* He told them there is no right or wrong way to finish the sentence, and that he's only interested in their associations. Tony also indicated that they would be reading their completions aloud and cautioned them about writing something that's too personal.

Next he asked everyone to share his or her sentence with the group. Answers included *"inevitable,"* *"hard to resist,"* and *"a voice inside me coaxing me to do something I know is wrong."* Then he gave the following remarks to provide transition into the Bible study:

In This Chapter...

- Introducing a Bible study
- Organizing questions and notes
- Concluding the Bible study
- The sequence of questions

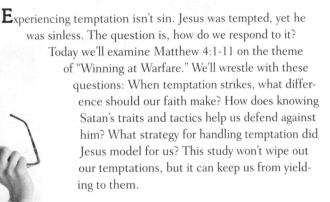

Experiencing temptation isn't sin. Jesus was tempted, yet he was sinless. The question is, how do we respond to it? Today we'll examine Matthew 4:1-11 on the theme of "Winning at Warfare." We'll wrestle with these questions: When temptation strikes, what difference should our faith make? How does knowing Satan's traits and tactics help us defend against him? What strategy for handling temptation did Jesus model for us? This study won't wipe out our temptations, but it can keep us from yielding to them.

Why did Tony start the study time in this manner? Why didn't he delve into the passage immediately? He displayed a keen sensitivity to the organization of the Bible discussion. He thought of an introduction that whetted their appetite for the study and showed everyone its relevance to their lives.

In this chapter I'll identify the basic parts to a sound discussion plan and show you a logical sequence for structuring your Bible-study time. You'll discover a format that gets group members into God's Word and gets God's Word into them. You'll see how the various types of discussion questions fit into the structure.

Most publishers of leader's guides follow an organization pattern similar to this one. Their terminology for lesson parts differs, but their process follows the same educationally sound outline.

APPROACH
THE WORD

PARTS OF A
PRACTICAL
DISCUSSION

ABSORB
THE WORD

APPLY
THE WORD

APPROACH THE WORD

Folks come to a small group meeting operating at varying wavelengths. Though they've chosen to attend, it isn't safe to assume their minds are on the upcoming Bible discussion. Sally feels uptight about a recent argument with her teenage daughter. Bill is dragging from lack of sleep. Jane and Randy are on the lookout for their best friends who are members of the group. Mike is preoccupied with a conflict he's having at work. The Smiths' grown son is on their minds because he just lost his job.

Numerous inner factors, usually unknown to the leader, operate within group members. Since other people or personal circumstances claim their attention, it's difficult for them to jump right into a Bible lesson. In view of human nature, a wise discussion facilitator plans to "Approach the Word" before investigating it.

What should this opening segment accomplish? Whatever you do or say should lead group members to think about the topic or passage theme. Begin with a life-related activity that makes people leave their train of thought and focus instead on the subject of the study. Rather than assume people's interest, you earn it.

TRY THIS!

Examine a published leader's guide or teacher's manual that provides a start-to-finish lesson plan, one that outlines what the group leader should do and say in sequence. Compare the flow or structure to the suggested format in this chapter. This comparison will enable you to grasp the organizational pattern for a Bible study without being tied to particular terminology.

WiSe Words

"Adult learners need to see the immediate usefulness of new learning. Most adults do not have time to waste. We want to spend our time studying content that will make a difference now."

—Jane Vella, Learning to Listen, Learning to Teach

Grab group members' attention by raising a question, referring to a problem, or introducing an issue that's relevant to them and that is addressed in the Bible passage. Your "Approach the Word" should tap into some felt need within learners and give them a reason for paying attention. An approach activity is brief, usually three-to-five minutes. It should increase anticipation for the study and lead smoothly and logically into the Bible passage for the day.

Tony's introduction to Matthew 4:1-11 is a case in point. He created identification with the topic, because everyone

Now That's A Good Question! **65**

wrestles with temptation. Also notice how he provided clear transition into the passage. He constructed a "verbal bridge" that showed the connection between the sentence completion and the Bible study. You don't have to write it out, but I do recommend thinking through your transitional remarks in advance, so the shift from your introduction to the Bible passage is smooth and clear.

You can select from a wide range of methods: questions, illustrations, word associations, object lessons, thought-provoking quotations, humor, and sentence completions. Vary your approach from week to week, making sure it accomplishes its purposes.

Here's another example of an "Approach the Word" segment.

Pam launched her ladies' Bible study by displaying a thermometer. She explained that one's body temperature is a vital sign of physical health. If a young child acts cranky and mopes around, we pop a thermometer into her mouth. If her temp is elevated, it's a sign of trouble within the body. Some sort of infection has set in. Then Pam posed a question: "How are our tongues like thermometers?"

The respondents pointed out that words are an indicator of spiritual health. Next, Pam offered the following transition into the Bible study:

I've titled today's Bible study "The Thermometer of the Heart." In Luke 6:45, Jesus said that a person speaks "out of the overflow of his heart." Just as body temperature is a vital sign of physical health, our speech patterns are a vital sign of our spiritual health. What practical guidelines does God offer as a reference point for evaluating our daily conversations? How can we use the tongue to help others instead of harm them? Let's turn to a verse that addresses these questions: Ephesians 4:29.

Extra! Extra!

Though it comes first in my group Bible discussion, my preparation for this "Approach the Word" segment often comes last—after I've finished my study of the passage and after I've prepared my study questions. The better I grasp the passage's teaching, the easier it is to think of a way to introduce it. There's more fuel for my brainstorming that way.

Whether you call it an introduction, hook, focusing activity, lesson launch, or approach, the opening segment serves as an impetus for exploring the passage.

Super-Size It!

The marker board at the front of most classrooms is a useful tool for the "Approach the Word" lesson segment. Before learners enter write on the board a question or thought-provoking statement. They see the remark or question when they arrive, and their curiosity is aroused. For example, before a lesson on money from 1 Timothy 6, you might write, "Have you ever seen a hearse pulling a U-haul?" To launch a study on the tongue, seek answers to the following question, which has already been written on the board: "Who can illustrate the power of words to either help or hurt?" Before a lesson on 2 Timothy 4 on Paul's impending death, write on the board, "Cemeteries are filled with indispensable people."

ABSORB THE WORD

Absorb: To take in and make a part of one's being.

See the definition of absorb? That's precisely your goal during a Bible study! You want group members' exposure to Scripture to result in their assimilation of it. That's why you devote a majority of your meeting time to direct investigation of a Bible passage. The group Bible discussion is a natural extension of the introduction. Group members' attention shifts to God's perspectives on the issue, problem, or question you raised during the "Approach the Word" segment.

During this "Absorb the Word" phase of the study, participants experience the observation and interpretation steps of the Bible study. You familiarize them with what the passage says. You guide them to timeless truths implied or illustrated by the factual content.

Crack open leader's guides offered by Christian publishers, and you'll uncover a variety of terms for this investigative phase of the lesson—Lesson Development, Explore, Discover, and Bible Learning, to name a few. No matter how you label it, this section outlines a step-by-step strategy for covering Bible content.

Now That's A Good Question! **67**

As a discussion leader, you'll prompt their investigation of Scripture with a combination of observation and interpretation questions. To put the finishing touches on this "Absorb the Word" segment of your discussion plan, here's a sequential approach.

1 Identify the important facts and truths you need to cover during the group meeting.

2 Write discussion questions that will enable group members to find key facts and articulate the principles.

3 Jot down your own answer to each question you formulate. (Recording what you perceive to be ideal responses has two advantages. First, you'll be ready to supplement group members' contributions with insights of your own. That's especially helpful when questions have two or more possible answers. Second, your detailed notes will come in handy if you lead a study on this passage again. You'll save time because you won't reexamine the text to find answers long forgotten.)

4 Decide if you need any lecture material that corresponds with specific truths or supplements learner responses to questions. Place those notes at the appropriate place in your discussion plan. In your written plan, you might insert a key word, phrase, or Bible verse that will remind you of what you want to say. These notes can be in skeletal form and won't take up a lot of space on the paper. Then insert this material right after you discuss a question on a particular point.

The "Absorb the Word" section consists of everything you plan to do, say, or ask, arranged in the order in which you envision it occurring.

Remember Pam's lesson on "The Thermometer of the Heart"? The "Absorb the Word" segment of her discussion plan focused on Ephesians 4:29: *"Do not let any unwholesome talk come out of your mouths, but only what is helpful for building others up according to their needs, that it may benefit those who listen."*

This is a simple verse that doesn't require observation questions, so Pam zeroed in on a single interpretation assignment. She instructed the ladies to work with a partner and jot down answers to this question: *"What guidelines for daily conversation can we glean from this verse?"* She told them to base their guidelines on key words in the verse and to state each guideline in the form of a question for reflection and self-evaluation. Each pair shared their guidelines ten minutes later. Pam complimented their input and then contributed her own guidelines prepared in advance:

Caution!

Lecture material does not mean long monologues, but one or two minute segments consisting of cross-references, word studies, personal illustrations, or essential background information on doctrinal terms and hard-to-understand verses.

➤ *Are any of my words unwholesome?*
➤ *Do my words build up or tear down other people?*
➤ *Do my words meet needs?*
➤ *What benefit do my words give to those I'm talking to or about?*

As she proceeded through her guidelines, Pam pointed out that "unwholesome" can also be translated "impure" or "unfit." To supplement the mandate to build others up with words, she referred to Proverbs 16:24: *"Pleasant words are a honeycomb, sweet to the soul and healing to the bones."* Pam described a time when another Christian's words had encouraged her and restored her faith in God. She wrapped up their coverage of the speech criteria with another cross-reference that mentions the prevalence of tongue sins: *"When words are many, sin is not absent, but he who holds his tongue is wise"* (Proverbs 10:19).

Pam's interpretation question, word study, recap of the discussion in the form of

TRY THIS!

When you put together a discussion plan, pay close attention to the visual layout. Your questions should stand out so you can see them at a glance. Use white space liberally, and put questions in boldface or all caps so you don't have to look for them among your notes. This enables you to maintain better eye contact with the group and assures that you don't lose your place as you proceed through the questions.

her own guidelines, the two cross-references, and the personal anecdote were the components of her "Absorb the Word" segment. The ladies experienced the joy of discovering truth, while at the same time benefiting from Pam's preparation.

APPLY THE WORD

As emphasized in chapter 4, you'll devote part of your group meeting to life-related questions. Together, you'll probe the practical implications of material that you observe and interpret. By planning an "Apply the Word" segment, you're acknowledging that behavior change—not knowledge—is the ultimate purpose of Bible study.

Why insert a separate section on application into your discussion plan? If you don't plan to discuss a lesson's life implications, other group activities or coverage of content will consume all the meeting time. A section labeled "Apply the Word" serves as a visible reminder to emphasize it. Also, many learners don't discern potential responses to God's truth on their own. They need group interaction to stimulate their thinking. The questions and anecdotes help them connect Bible truth to their own circumstances.

As in the "Absorb the Word" segment, crafting this section requires listing in succession the questions you plan to ask. How long you spend in the "Apply the Word" part of the study depends on the nature of your Bible passage, the needs or background of group members, and the total amount of time you have for the meeting. In most cases, at least 25% of your total group time should be spent on this "Apply the Word" segment.

To illustrate an "Apply the Word" segment, here are the questions Pam asked after participants identified the conversational guidelines from Ephesians 4:29.

➤ *In what kind of situations are we prone to use "unwholesome" speech?*

➤ *What are some examples of words that build up others spiritually?*

➤ *Who can share a time when a need was met by another person's words?*

➤ *Often we talk to others about a third party who isn't present. How can we keep such conversations from degenerating into gossip?*

To conclude her "Apply the Word" segment, Pam asked the following rhetorical questions and then followed them with a couple minutes of silent prayer.

➤ *What relationships came to mind as we identified the speech guidelines in Ephesians 4:29? (Pause.)*

➤ *Why did God's Spirit bring those people to mind? Is there someone you've sinned against, from whom you need to seek forgiveness? Or did you think of someone who needs the encouragement your words can offer? (Pause.)*

➤ *Look over the conversational criteria again. To be in conformity to God's Word, which guideline do you most need to incorporate into your daily conversations? (Pause.)*

SWITCH THE SEQUENCE

If you glanced at Pam's written discussion plan, you'd see her interpretation questions and list of answers are under a section labeled "Absorb the Word," and her application questions would be in the "Apply the Word" section. Often that's a natural approach to organizing your questions: list the observation and interpretation assignments and then conclude with all the application inquiries. In such a format, all life-related questions are set apart from the Bible-discovery segment.

Sometimes, however, it's more effective to employ a few application questions within the "Absorb the Word" part of the lesson. Rather than reserve all life-related inquiries for a separate segment, follow the observation-interpretation-application pattern on a given truth or verse. Then move to a different passage element and start over again with either observation or interpretation exercises.

Questions and anecdotes help participants connect Bible truths to their own lives.

In the exploration of Ephesians 4:29, as soon as a group member cited a guideline on "building up others," Pam could have inserted this life-related question: *"What are some examples of words that build up others spiritually?"* She didn't have to wait

Now That's A Good Question! **71**

until all the guidelines were identified before exploring application of this particular criteria for conversations.

Another example will help clarify what I mean. In an exploration of Jesus' temptations in Matthew 4:1-11, here's a sequence of questions you could ask. Notice how a life-related question on one point is inserted before covering a different principle.

> **Interpretation**— *What did Jesus model for us about handling temptation?*
>
> **Life-Related**— *Who can illustrate how God's Word sustains or assists us in a time of spiritual warfare?*
>
> **Interpretation**— *Satan tempted Jesus three times, not just once. What does that fact tell us about Satan?*

Switching the sequence of questions does not erase the need for a separate "Apply the Word" lesson segment. It's still a top-shelf priority to reserve time for personal reflection on the passage as a whole. Mixing in a few life-related questions simply means you probe practical points as they crop up rather than reserving all application questions for the concluding segment.

In this chapter, you've learned how to organize a discussion plan for leading a Bible study. What follows is a start-to-finish discussion plan that illustrates the format I've been

TRY THIS
TEAMWORK IDEA!

Have each group member share the title of a magazine that describes his or her life over the past few weeks. Ask participants to explain the reason for their selection. Spur their thinking with these examples.

- **Decision:** "I'm wrestling with the possibility of changing jobs."

- **Time:** "I haven't had enough of it lately due to heavier demands at work."

- **Money:** "Things are tight since we started a fund for our kids' college education."

Pray together for the needs and burdens revealed by the periodical titles.

describing. It's the same passage you used in previous chapters to practice writing Bible-study questions.

Discussion Plan for Philippians 1:1-11
"How Christian Fellowship Shows"

1Paul and Timothy, servants of Christ Jesus, To all the saints in Christ Jesus at Philippi, together with the overseers and deacons: 2Grace and peace to you from God our Father and the Lord Jesus Christ. 3I thank my God every time I remember you. 4In all my prayers for all of you, I always pray with joy 5because of your partnership in the gospel from the first day until now, 6being confident of this, that he who began a good work in you will carry it on to completion until the day of Christ Jesus. 7It is right for me to feel this way about all of you, since I have you in my heart; for whether I am in chains or defending and confirming the gospel, all of you share in God's grace with me. 8God can testify how I long for all of you with the affection of Christ Jesus. 9And this is my prayer: that your love may abound more and more in knowledge and depth of insight, 10so that you may be able to discern what is best and may be pure and blameless until the day of Christ, 11filled with the fruit of righteousness that comes through Jesus Christ—to the glory and praise of God.

Theme Statement: *Philippians 1:1-11 offers timeless expressions of Christian fellowship.*

Approach the Word

What do you associate with the word fellowship? Transition into Bible Lesson: We've expressed what we associate with the word fellowship, and we've shared some of our experiences. But it is even more important to know what God associates with the word. From God's perspective, what does genuine fellowship look like? What type of things does he want us to experience in our relationships with other Christians? We can find answers to those questions in Paul's introduction to the book of Philippians. Let's turn to Philippians 1:1-11 and find timeless expressions of fellowship that should describe our relationships too.

Absorb the Word

Lecture: Give two to three minutes of background on the letter of Philippians. Review how the Philippian church was founded, using information in Acts 16, and how close relationships started between Paul's team and people like Lydia and the jailer. Mention that Paul wrote the Philippian letter from prison in Rome, primarily to thank them for their prayers and for a financial contribution they made to his ministry (see Philippians 4:14-16). Refer to 1:5, where Paul mentioned "your partnership in the gospel." The word partnership is the word koinonia, which is also translated "fellowship."

Discussion:

Observation: *Paul used the word servant to describe himself and Timothy (v. 1).*

Interpretation: *What does that word tell us about their attitudes and their purpose in life?* (It means they considered themselves the property of Christ. They were at his complete disposal, fully committed to him. Their purpose was to serve him by telling others about him.)

Interpretation: *How does our commitment to the Lord affect the quality of fellowship with other believers?* (Only God can give us unselfish hearts and unconditional love for others. Closeness to others depends on intimacy with the Lord.)

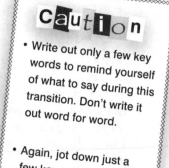

Caution

• Write out only a few key words to remind yourself of what to say during this transition. Don't write it out word for word.

• Again, jot down just a few key words to remind yourself what to say.

Interpretation: *How would you describe the mood, or emotional atmosphere, of verses 3-11?* (warm, friendly, positive, thankful)

Observation: *What words or phrases from this passage show that Paul and the Philippians enjoyed a close relationship?*

v. 3: "I thank my God every time I remember you."
v. 4: "all my prayers for all of you"
v. 5: "your partnership in the gospel"
v. 7: "to feel this way about all of you"
v. 7: "I have you in my heart."
v. 8: "I long for all of you with the affection of Christ Jesus."

Interpretation: Divide into pairs. Take five or six minutes to work together and identify answers to this question: "What timeless expressions of fellowship did Paul and the Philippians model for us?" After several minutes, reconvene and ask volunteers to share answers with the whole group. Supplement their answers as needed from the following list.

At this point in the study, give a longer "interpretation" assignment. Now that they are familiar with the passage, help them to identify principles about fellowship or look for timeless expressions of fellowship illustrated in those verses.

➤ *Write letters when physically separated to offer encouragement and counsel (Paul wrote them!)*
➤ *Exercise ministry of intercessory prayer for one another (vv. 4, 9–11)*
➤ *Give to meet material needs (the Philippians gave money to Paul; implied in v. 5)*
➤ *Openly express affection instead of taking positive feelings for granted (vv. 7, 8)*
➤ *Share experiences and time together, which is crucial to developing fellowship (v. 3: "every time I remember you" referred to events recorded in Acts 16)*

Apply the Word

Life-Related: *We've examined expressions of fellowship in Philippians 1:1-11. In what additional ways can fellowship show?*

Life-Related: *What are some hindrances in our culture to experiencing this sort of fellowship?*

Life-Related: *Who will share a time when you've been on the receiving end of one of these forms of fellowship?*

APPLICATION PROJECT

Think about the ways fellowship was displayed between Paul and the Philippians. Decide on one thing you can do this week to express concern for or initiate fellowship with an individual or a group of believers. (Answers could include writing someone an encouraging letter, helping a struggling believer financially, or beginning a ministry of intercession for a brother in need.) Close in a time of silent prayer, asking God to help you take the initiative with someone.

A skillful discussion leader also knows what to do after he or she poses a question. Chapter 7 shows you how to respond to group members and improve the quality of their responses.

TRY THIS!

Use the discussion plan on Philippians 1:1-11 with your group. Examining this passage together may enhance your corporate experience of fellowship.

BRINGING IT HOME

➤ *Introduce your Bible study in an interesting way. Show the relevance of the passage before you examine it together.*

➤ *Write study questions and any related supplementary notes in the order you plan to cover them.*

➤ *Close with questions to help group members personalize the passage and apply it to their lives.*

➤ *Possibly weave life-related questions into your "Absorb the Word" segment of the discussion plan. It isn't necessary for all application questions to come at the end.*

Facilitating Lively Discussions

Let's listen in on a conversation between a kindergartner and his dad.

Who made God?

Nobody made God. He has always been alive.

But, how did he get borned?

God isn't like us. He did not have to be born. He never had a beginning.

But ... but who made him?

This is very hard to understand, isn't it? There are many things about God I don't understand yet. All I know is that God was alive before anything else, and he wasn't born like you or me.

But how did he get hisself?

In This Chapter...

- Responding to group members' participation
- Positive reinforcement techniques
- Wait time
- Follow-up questions
- Expanding participation

Whether you are a parent or teach kids in Sunday school, the young ones keep you on our toes with their curiosity. How you respond to their questions is crucial in your attempts to influence them.

How a discussion leader responds to group members' inquiries is also important. Their questions won't tax you as much as the kindergartner's probe. But what you say and do when they pose a question either enhances or stifles further group interaction.

Now That's A Good Question! **77**

Responding to their questions is just one of a number of discussion-leading skills you'll need to cultivate. Other competencies have to do with your reaction to their answers to questions. This chapter examines a taken-for-granted aspect of discussion-leading.

Let's explore ways to respond to group members' participation.

EXHIBIT ENTHUSIASM

A leader's behavior after posing questions is a hinge upon which first-rate discussion turns.

When you lead quality Bible discussions, people find fresh, I've-never-thought-of-that-before insights. In response to a study question, participants may notice a truth for the very first time, especially if they're recent converts. Then they verbalize their discovery for others to hear. This is the time to reward their participation with positive reinforcement. Express excitement over their discoveries as if each one is new to you.

What you say right after someone contributes is crucial. If her point is elementary to you or something you've known for years, you may gloss over it or give it only polite acknowledgement. But your verbal reaction should express fascination with the participant's discovery! I'm not advocating mushy, superficial remarks or positive reinforcement of an incorrect response. But I am encouraging you to speak a few sentences that dignify legitimate answers. Give verbal applause that recognizes a person's textual investigation. Public congratulations

> *When someone makes a contribution, I say 'Fantastic, thank you!' Or 'I think in all the years I've been studying the Bible I've never seen that insight from this passage.' You celebrate what they say. Make a hero out of anyone who contributes.*
>
> *—Howard Hendricks, Teaching to Change Lives*

will encourage people to keep delving into Scripture and participating in the discussion. Help them build confidence in their study skills and convince them that God's Spirit can unveil biblical truth to them.

SHOW SINCERITY

Here's the flip side of the positive reinforcement coin. Temper your enthusiasm in relation to the quality of a group member's answer. Indiscriminate praise without regard to the quality of their answers backfires because your commendations come across as insincere. Group members hesitate to give serious thought to a question if you treat every answer the same. So reserve the highest praise for the best answers or for feedback that reveals critical thinking on the issue you're discussing. Also be sure to praise participants for thought-provoking questions they raise and for input that shows an honest effort to wrestle with the text.

Verbal applause will encourage group members to keep delving into Scripture and participating in the discussion!

One way to show sincerity is to make your positive reinforcement as specific as possible. Which part of a group member's response hit the bull's-eye? Notice how the following reinforcements shine the spotlight on distinctive aspects of learner contributions.

✦ "Excellent answer, Valerie. I like the way you referred to Jesus' words to support your conclusions."

✦ "That's a provocative question, Joseph. Sometimes our zeal for God's Word shows more in the questions we ask than in the answers we give."

✦ "Way to go, Bryan! You did a good job of putting Paul's remark in context."

✦ "Beth, that's good thinking. Could you repeat your answer so we can think about it a little more?" (Turn to others in the group.) "Notice how Beth unites these two episodes. The connection isn't obvious at first glance."

- "It's evident you fellows don't see eye-to-eye on this issue. But I appreciate the way you expressed your viewpoints tactfully and listened to each other."
- "I'm impressed by the way you connected this verse to last week's lesson."

By pointing out particular elements within learners' remarks, you motivate them to keep participating. You prove that you listened carefully to what was said.

WIN WITH WAITING

Brad peppers his Bible study with thought-provoking questions. That's why the absence of stimulating discussion in his group puzzles him. What answers he receives are terse. Seldom does anyone piggyback on the first response.

"Why aren't they more responsive?" Brad wonders aloud during a breakfast appointment with David. David, Brad's best friend and a member of the group, decides to shoot straight with him.

"You specialize in questions that involve the intellect," David explains. "They're so analytical that it takes a little while to investigate the Bible passage and come up with answers. Not even your application questions are obvious. We have to reflect on personal experiences before coming up with ideas."

"But that sounds like a compliment," interrupted Brad.

"So far so good," David continued. "But I don't think you're aware of how little time you give us to think after you pose a question. No more than a couple of seconds pass before you answer it yourself. Brad, you've already thought about your questions during the week. But the rest of us haven't. Just yesterday you asked about the difference between remorse and repentance. I had read something on the subject, and my mind was busy formulating a response. Then before I could verbalize it, you dropped your research on us. I'd be less than honest if I didn't say that it siphoned off my enthusiasm."

Increasing the "wait time" after posing a question has several advantages:

Learners volunteer more accurate responses.

Their answers reveal better reasoning and more analytical thinking.

More participants respond to the question.

Participants are more likely to ask questions of their own about the topic.

TRY THIS!

Instruct group members to take a specified amount of time before responding orally to a Bible-study question. After asking the question, say something like, "Take thirty seconds to think about it before you answer." Or, "I'm giving you a couple minutes to examine the passage before I'll accept responses." Then let them know when time is up. This approach alleviates the discomfort some folks feel when there's silence during a discussion.

When you pose a question, how long do you wait before answering it yourself or rephrasing it? How many seconds elapse before you feel obligated to get things moving? Do you view silence as a threat to effective discussion? Discussion leaders tend to answer questions themselves if no one responds within three to five seconds. But it often takes learners longer than that to examine a Bible passage and formulate a response.

A way to lower the amount of "wait time" that's needed is to have learners read verses on which a question is based before you ask it. Say something like, "The next few questions are based on verses 6-12. Read those verses carefully before we examine them together." Then pose the questions. Their familiarity with what the passage says expedites the interaction.

NOTICE THE NONVERBAL

While leading a women's Bible study, Betty posed a question about secrets to contentment. The second she finished the probe, Betty shifted her eyes away from the group members to the notes in her lap. Elaine started to say something, but her interest evaporated when she noticed Betty's preoccupation with her notes. After a few seconds of silence, Betty looked up and answered the question herself, referring to a specific verse for support. Elaine had seen the same point in the text, and she had planned to illustrate it from her own experience.

Betty's poor eye contact hindered interaction. Whether you're engaged in a casual conversation or leading a Bible study, your communication comes

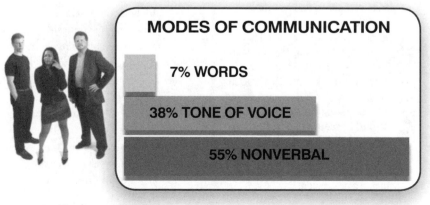

MODES OF COMMUNICATION

7% WORDS

38% TONE OF VOICE

55% NONVERBAL

across through three modes: actual words, tone of voice, and nonverbal cues. To maximize effectiveness, package your message in a way that utilizes all three avenues of expression.

You may be surprised at how little impact words themselves make. Experts on communication theory insist that how you say something packs more of a wallop than what you say. In a conversation or teaching situation, 7% of your message is conveyed through words, 38% through tone of voice, and 55% through nonverbal signals (Richard Peace and Thom Corrigan, Learning to Care: Developing Community in Small Groups).

During discussion time, when is your nonverbal communication most potent? *When others are talking!* As participants answer or ask questions, what message is your body language sending? Do you come across as tense or relaxed? interested or impatient? What you say without speaking can either fan the flames of group participation or throw icy water on them.

Educational researchers compared the relative effects of verbal and nonverbal reinforcement in response to student comments. On

TRY THIS
TEAMWORK IDEA!

Divide the group into pairs. Give each person two minutes to introduce himself to his or her partner—without using words. The partner may speak, guessing what the communicator is trying to say nonverbally. After two minutes, switch and give the other person a chance to introduce himself the same way. Next, instruct each pair to join another twosome. Then give everyone two minutes to introduce his partner to the new pair—nonverbally, of course. Before you reconvene, tell each foursome to talk about their nonverbal experience.

Use the nonverbal introductions as a springboard for a discussion of communication patterns in small groups. Ask these questions: What did you learn about interpersonal communication from this activity? What nonverbal messages do members of groups often send? What examples of negative nonverbal cues can you cite? What positive nonverbal cues enhance the relational climate of a group? How can awareness of each other's nonverbal messages improve our ministry to one another?

one occasion, college teachers sent conflicting reinforcement messages as a way of determining which mode students perceived as more powerful.

In one group, the teacher displayed positive nonverbal reinforcement (smiled, maintained eye contact, indicated positive attitude to students' answers with facial and body cues), but at the same time sent out negative verbal messages. In the second case, the process was reversed, and negative nonverbal reinforcement was coupled with positive verbal reinforcement (frowns, poor eye contact, and the like coupled with "good," "nice job," and so forth).

In both cases the majority of students accepted the nonverbal reinforcement as the teacher's primary message. Whether the nonverbal message was positive or negative, most students responded to the nonverbal rather than to the verbal reinforcement (from Myra and David Sadker, "Questioning Skills" in Classroom Teaching Skills).

> ### Super-Size It!
> Here's a simple technique I use to convince class members that I'm interested in their questions and contributions. When a person starts speaking, I move to a spot in the classroom that's closer to them. If a person to my left speaks up, I take a few steps so I'm standing in front of people to my left. If a person near the back says something, I take a few steps forward. I don't do this because I have trouble hearing. It's a nonverbal signal that says, "I'm listening. Your participation is important to me."

Responding to a group member's questions or input is "the art of the immediate." It's hard to prepare for because your response requires a number of complex, on-the-spot decisions. It's as much a relational skill as it is a teaching proficiency. Yet with prayerful effort, you can transmit appropriate, positive nonverbal messages as you lead. Consider the following aspects of your nonverbal delivery system.

The LORD bless you and keep you; the LORD make his face shine upon you and be gracious to you.
—Numbers 6:24, 25

➤ Body movement and posture: If you're sitting in a circle, lean forward or inch closer to the edge of your chair whenever others contribute. They'll feel that you're listening with your heart, not just your ears.

➤ Facial Expressions and Eye Contact: In the Bible, one's "face" often represents the whole person, whether human or divine. When God's face shined upon Israel, he was blessing them. When he turned his face away, he was withdrawing his favor. Why did the Holy Spirit use "face" as a metaphor for the sentiments of the heart? Perhaps it was because without the aid of words, one's face usually expresses his inner convictions or condition.

When your group members participate in a discussion, does your face convey boredom or enthusiasm? Do you nod to let them know you're following their line of thought? Do you rivet your eyes to the person who's talking or shift them back and forth between the participant and your notes? You may hear everything a group member says without looking at him, but listening requires eye contact.

TRY THIS!

Yogi Berra quipped, "You can observe a lot by watching." Apply his maxim to your leadership role. Observe your group members closely when they arrive at the group session, as they participate in the meeting, and as they mingle during less structured social times. Notice their facial expressions. Are they smiling or downcast? What does their posture suggest about their energy level or physical well-being? Do they establish and keep eye contact during conversations? Do their eyes convey enthusiasm? discouragement? weariness? Is someone who's normally jovial and expressive now reticent? Ask the Holy Spirit to make you sensitive to needs that are expressed nonverbally.

You may hear everything a group member says without looking at him, but listening requires eye contact.

FOLLOW UP THEIR FEEDBACK

Not all answers to your Bible-study questions are fully developed. Often a group member is onto something, but his comment needs clarification. Or what she says is fine as far as it goes, but it needs elaboration. Follow responses of this sort with probing questions. Your follow-up probes should spur

Now That's A Good Question! **85**

a group member to modify or expand his initial answer, beef up its support, illustrate it, or think more critically about it.

Probing for extensions of original answers is challenging. You need on-the-spot sensitivity because you can't prepare follow-up questions or comments in advance. Yet just being aware that follow-up questions can be helpful is a start toward using them.

Here's a script from a Bible discussion that demonstrates the effectiveness of follow-up prompts. Notice that the leader doesn't blindly accept the initial answer. Questions in *italics* were prepared in advance by the leader. Underlined questions and comments indicate follow-up material inserted on the spot.

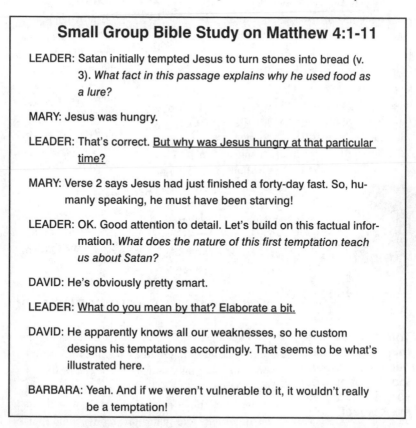

Small Group Bible Study on Matthew 4:1-11

LEADER: Satan initially tempted Jesus to turn stones into bread (v. 3). *What fact in this passage explains why he used food as a lure?*

MARY: Jesus was hungry.

LEADER: That's correct. But why was Jesus hungry at that particular time?

MARY: Verse 2 says Jesus had just finished a forty-day fast. So, humanly speaking, he must have been starving!

LEADER: OK. Good attention to detail. Let's build on this factual information. *What does the nature of this first temptation teach us about Satan?*

DAVID: He's obviously pretty smart.

LEADER: What do you mean by that? Elaborate a bit.

DAVID: He apparently knows all our weaknesses, so he custom designs his temptations accordingly. That seems to be what's illustrated here.

BARBARA: Yeah. And if we weren't vulnerable to it, it wouldn't really be a temptation!

LEADER: You've both identified an important characteristic of our enemy. He tempts us with things that obviously have appeal. He knows everyone's vulnerability, spiritually speaking. Let's see what else the episode tells us about the devil. *Notice that he tempted Jesus three times, not just once. What is significant about that fact?*

JOSEPH: Well, resisting the devil isn't a one-time thing. It's something we have to keep doing all our lives.

LEADER: Absolutely right, Joseph. <u>But what does that imply about Satan?</u>

JOSEPH: He doesn't give up easily, that's for sure.

BARBARA: Another way to put it is he's persistent.

LEADER: Exactly! That's why a word picture of the Christian life is warfare. Let's keep unpacking this point. *If Satan is persistent, how should that affect us as believers?*

MARY: We need to be persistent too. Or else we're in trouble. We won't be ready to defend against him.

LEADER: Mary, you hit the bull's-eye by pointing out the basic application of this fact about Satan. But let's get more specific. <u>How does persistence show in the life of a Christian?</u>

WiSe Words

"Passive exposure to information through reading or hearing a lecture has less effect on people's attitudes than when they get the same information through active participation in a group discussion."

—David Myers, Quoted in Bill McNabb and Steven Mabry, *Teaching the Bible Creatively*

In a span of several minutes, the leader employed four different follow-up probes that led to increased interaction among group members and deeper understanding and application.

More Examples

The range of possible follow-up questions is broad, depending on the context of the discussion. Let the following examples serve as additional catalysts for your thinking.

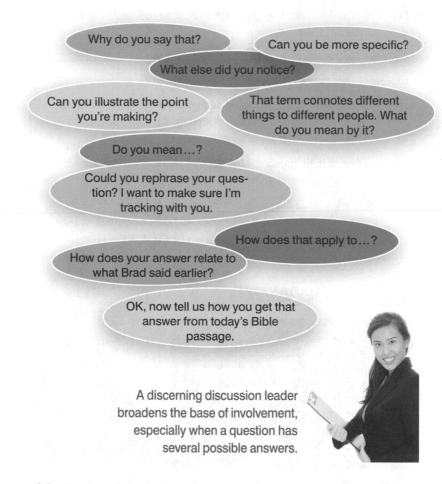

Why do you say that?

Can you be more specific?

What else did you notice?

Can you illustrate the point you're making?

That term connotes different things to different people. What do you mean by it?

Do you mean...?

Could you rephrase your question? I want to make sure I'm tracking with you.

How does that apply to...?

How does your answer relate to what Brad said earlier?

OK, now tell us how you get that answer from today's Bible passage.

A discerning discussion leader broadens the base of involvement, especially when a question has several possible answers.

EXTRA! EXTRA!

For more help on dealing with a variety of challenges as you lead discussion, see the Small Group HELP! Guide, *Why Didn't You Warn Me?* by Pat Sikora (Standard Publishing). It's a great companion guide to this book!

Increase Involvement

Some discussions are nothing more than a question-and-answer dialog between the leader and one other participant. Only one volunteer responds to a question before the leader kicks in with either commentary or the next question. Or a group member poses a question, and no one but the designated leader addresses it. Rarely do you hear a second participant piggyback on the initial answer someone gives. It's as if people are afraid to trespass on the leader's domain of expertise.

A discerning discussion leader broadens the base of involvement, especially when a question has several possible answers or during a brainstorming session

INTERACTION PATTERNS

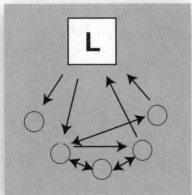

1. Participants respond to one another, not just the leader. Leader is a facilitator.

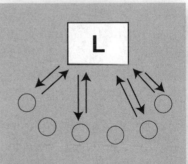

2. Two-way conversations between leader and one other group member. Leader is considered the only expert in the group.

on application ideas. She often encourages multiple responses to a question before adding her own research or going on to the next question. When a participant asks a question, a good leader often taps the wisdom of others by redirecting the question to them. The more mature and biblically literate your group, the more you should strive to expand participation.

Before you supplement a group member's answer or tackle someone's question yourself, increase involvement and interest by asking questions similar to the following:

> *Would someone else like to address Bob's question?*

> *What do the rest of you think?*

> *Bob, you seem puzzled by Stan's comment. What's your reaction to what he said? (Normally, I direct a question to individuals only when their expression warrants it.)*

> *Jenny identified an important principle in this chapter. Who can illustrate the consequences of either obeying it or neglecting it in our relationships?*

> *I appreciate your transparency, Myra. Your question stems from a sincere desire to honor the Lord in that situation. Who has a biblical perspective or personal experience that can help Myra sort out her Christian responsibility in this predicament?*

> *Who can identify with what Sally is saying?*

BRINGING IT HOME

➤ Your behavior after posing a question is an important factor for discussion.

➤ Give positive reinforcement to group members' answers as well as to their questions.

➤ Be aware of the nonverbal messages you send.

➤ Deepen or improve learners' responses with follow-up questions.

➤ Increase involvement by letting others respond to a participant's question or contribution.

Remember:
God equips you for what he calls you to do.

Super-Size It!

When I'm in a more formal classroom setting, I put my notes or lesson plan on a small lectern or music stand. But I place it on either side of me, rather than stand behind it. I can still glance at it as needed. This method helps a leader to come across as more approachable and enhances learner involvement. Class members answer and ask more questions with no physical barrier between them and the teacher.

YOU CAN DO IT!

When you think about your role as a small group leader, don't cower before the responsibility. When I face a daunting task, I'm encouraged by God's promise of his presence. I'm not alone in carrying out the task, and neither are you. What he pledged to the people of Israel is true for you and me: *"So do not fear, for I am with you; do not be dismayed, for I am your God. I will strengthen you and help you; I will uphold you with my righteous right hand"* (Isaiah 41:10). We may not always feel God's presence, but he is with us nonetheless. His Word is more reliable than our feelings!

Also let this truth buoy your spirit: God equips you for what he calls you to do. Resolve to do your part and implement the ideas in this book. Then God's enablement will supplement your effort, "for it is God who works in you to will and to act according to his good purpose" (Philippians 2:13).

If teaching were only telling, my kids would be incredibly brilliant.
—Howard Hendricks, Teaching to Change Lives

Small Group

EXTENSION ACTIVITIES

To encourage discussion in a more formal classroom setting, I often give "listening assignments" prior to a lecture segment. This increases learners' attention while I talk. When I finish, I solicit feedback on the assignments. I may tell the men, "Be ready to define justification in your own words." I may instruct the women to listen for answers to this question: "Despite our justified state before God, why does our behavior still matter?" I keep the assignments simple, limited to one key concept or thread of thought. They usually involve a review of key points or their application.

HUMOR WORKS!

In the chapter introductions to this book, I often employ humor. Share these anecdotes or excerpts with your group members. Spread them out so you use only one item in any given session. Material of this sort disarms folks and enhances the group atmosphere.

Occasionally your group may discuss a Christian book rather than passages right out of the Bible. Use questions similar to the following when you discuss the chapters:

* What was the author's main point in this chapter?
* What remark left the biggest impression on you? Why?
* What did the author say that you wish would have been elaborated on? Explain.
* How did the Holy Spirit speak a personal word to you as you read?
* If you have trouble accepting something the author said, tell why.

LIFE APPLICATION

When you're finishing a Bible-study series, use these questions to reflect on the experience. Give everyone a copy of the questions and let them choose any one of them to answer.

* How has the Lord encouraged or challenged you during this study?
* What one truth has the Lord impressed on you most? Why?
* Cite one person in the group that you've learned to appreciate and tell why.
* Tell us about one application you made from one of the Bible studies.

GROUP DYNAMICS

Christians in the church of Jerusalem changed Joseph's name to Barnabas, ("Son of Encouragement"). As a group, examine these passages: *Acts 4:32-37; 9:23-28; 11:19-26; and 15:36-41.* "Discuss: What conclusions about the ministry of encouragement can we gleam from these episodes? What forms can encouragement take within our group?"

CHECK OUT THIS VAUABLE COUPON!

FREE

SMALL GROUP RESOURCES

For MORE HELP, check out the small group leader resources on *SmallGroups.com*.

With the purchase of this book, you are entitled to a free one-month membership at *www.SmallGroups.com*. To claim your **FREE** membership:

➤ Go to: ***www.SmallGroups.com/freemembership*.**

➤ Continue through "checkout" process.

➤ Select payment method "check/money order." However, no payment is due if you use coupon code: **stdsg06**

➤ Then click "Redeem" and "Confirm Order" for your free membership!

Redeem your coupon *today!*